"*While You Were Gone: A Handbook for Returning Catholics* is a marvelous resource for understanding the Catholic Church in the 1990s. Fr. Bausch explains the changes in the celebration of the sacraments and church governance, and offers insights into the attitudes and behaviors of Catholics today. This information enables the returning Catholic to assess the spiritual desires of his or her heart and make an informed decision about how to live as an active and satisfied member of a parish family. Written by a wise and perceptive pastor who loves the Catholic faith, this book will help many returning Catholics (or those thinking about returning) to appreciate the opportunity of coming to know Christ better through the Catholic community of believers."

Rev. Kenneth Boyack, C.S.P., Director
The Paulist National Catholic Evangelization Association

"Father Bausch offers a clear, concise explanation of many of the changes that have occurred in the past twenty years in history, theology, ecclesiology, sociology, and culture—changes that have also affected the church. Obviously aware of and sensitive to the confusion that returning Catholics must feel, Bausch nevertheless offers them a critical look at controversial issues, offers practical guidelines for practicing the faith, and honestly welcomes them back to a less-than-perfect church. This is a rich resource for all returning Catholics . . . and a challenge for those who have never left!"

Susan W. Blum, Ed. D.
Director, Isaiah Parish Missions
Vice President, National Council for Catholic Evangelization

"*While You Were Gone* is an excellent book for those who have not been active in the church since the 1960s. Its down-to-earth approach is enhanced by its invitational style. Father Bill Bausch is, again, right on target providing a valuable resource for parishes who are reaching out and welcoming back those who have been away."

Dr. Maureen Gallagher, Ph.D.
(Milwaukee) Archbishop's Delegate for Parishes

D0103556

"Father Bausch here makes a major contribution to evangelization. With clarity and a conversational style, he explains changes in the church for returning Catholics and for those preparing for Catholicism. This is also a must-read for practicing Catholics who will understand and appreciate the rationale for change as they, too, extend a 'welcome home.'"

Patricia A. Yoczis
Writer, Reviewer

"Prayer is the way to get things started 'to come home to the church.' But frequently this will take some assurances that it is worth the effort. Pastor and prolific author William J. Bausch realized that many Catholics need help to support the good intentions of those who are contemplating returning to the church. *While You Were Gone* provides a marvelous resource for understanding the Catholic church in the 1990s. Here is factual support for people's prayerful efforts to help motivate friends and relatives 'to come home.'"

The Dialog
Wilmington, Delaware

"This book by the ever popular William J. Bausch deals with the changes that those who come home to the church will encounter, giving assurance that the essence of Catholicism remains constant. His chapters are brief, friendly, factual. Catholics who haven't left might also look to this book for an overview of changes in the church since Vatican II."

Rev. William C. Graham
National Catholic Reporter

"Father Bausch has written yet another practical pastoral work aimed at the key questions and concerns of Catholics pondering returning to the church after an absence of several years. Each chapter closes with an annotated list of suggested readings. Bausch, author of the most practical *The Hands-On Parish*, has again achieved exceptional practicality. Ideal for the Rite of Christian Initiation of Adults (R.C.I.A.), this book will serve well for both parish evangelization and outreach."

Msgr. Hugh J. Nolan
Catholic Standard & Times

WHILE YOU WERE GONE

A Handbook for Returning Catholics*

*and those thinking about it

WILLIAM J. BAUSCH

XXIII

TWENTY-THIRD PUBLICATIONS

Mystic, Connecticut 06355

For Sr. Frances Carmel
and all who have introduced me to the church
and kept reintroducing me
even when I might have fled

Second printing 1994

Twenty-Third Publications
185 Willow Street
P.O. Box 180
Mystic, CT 06355
(203) 536-2611
800-321-0411

ISBN 0-89622-575-5
Library of Congress Catalog Card Number 93-60817
Printed in the U.S.A.

CONTENTS

PART THREE—THE CHALLENGE

INTRODUCTION

According to a 1992 Gallup Poll, more and more Americans consider religion to be "very important" in their lives. According to the polls, too, more and more Americans are returning to organized religion, especially the Baby Boomers, those born between 1946 and 1962. Among these, of course, are Roman Catholics. Catholics have left the church in great numbers, but they are also returning in significant numbers: an estimated 320,000 each year.

The reasons for leaving and the reasons for returning are many and we shall discuss them in this book, but the returning itself poses its own challenges. Returning to one's hometown after a long absence, or returning to the class reunion (the only ones anxious for such class reunions, they say, are the rich and the thin) can leave one at bay and strangely off-center. So much has changed and it's hard getting used to it all. Or nothing has changed but *you* have, and it's hard to relate in the same way as when you were younger. In any case, some kind of map, some kind of reintro-

duction, some kind of guidance is in order for those returning to the Catholic church. Hence this book and its apt
title: *While You Were Gone.*

But this book also has in mind two other groups besides
those who have returned to the church. The first is those
who have not yet in fact returned, but are thinking about it.
Like the fox in *The Little Prince*, they are sitting at a distance,
looking at the church from the corner of their eye. They
were Catholics once and are wondering if they should give
it another try. It seems what they say is true: The church *is*
hard to get out of your system. Has anything changed that
might entice them back? For those who are considering this
step, this book might give them food for thought.

The second group that this book would help is catechumens, the ones preparing to become Catholics, those in
RCIA processes. The overview of the church, the dynamics
of history, the challenges of the present time as they are presented in this volume would be a useful guide for their journey.

This book is divided, like Gaul of old, into three parts.
Part One, "The Context," offers a wide view to the reader,
trying to give a sense that, yes, much has changed in the
Catholic church (you'll surely notice that), but those changes are not sudden, whimsical oddities of the Second Vatican
Council (1962-1965) but have deep roots in the happenings
of centuries and centuries before Pope John XXIII ever
thought of calling the council.

This part also describes how those happenings got translated in the way we were taught and the way we perceived
the church and the world. Finally, there's an inner context:
that of our first experiences of what it meant to be Catholic,
some pleasant and others horrific, but all impending on our
consciousness now.

Part Two, "The Changes," provides a quick overview of
those most obvious and public areas you are most likely to

encounter as a Catholic returning to the church: the changes in the Mass, the sacraments, the ministries, the parish, and Scripture.

Finally, Part Three, "The Challenge," offers an honest overview of some unfinished business in this church of ours (not surprising: We're all unfinished in some way or other) and invites us to stay steadfast on our journey.

I have tried to keep this book brief, conversational, and informative. For further reading, I have included a very select listing of books relating to the subject of each chapter, books that are short, readable, and enjoyable. I hope the returning Catholic will be moved to pursue what is suggested in this book.

I leave you with a quotation from one of the giants of the last century, Cardinal John Henry Newman. Although he was a convert, his words apply to you who have come back home:

> I have been in perfect peace and contentment; I never had one doubt to myself, on my conversion, of any change, intellectual or moral, wrought in my mind. I was not conscious of a firmer faith in the fundamental truths of revelation, or of more self-command; I had not more fervor; but it was like coming into a port after a rough sea; and my happiness on that score remains to this day without interruption.

Welcome back to the church, to this port after the storm. May your happiness increase and remain.

Part One

The Context

Chapter 1

ROOTS

Traumatizing Rip Van Winkle

If you are over 50, you would expect that a few things had changed when, like a religious Rip Van Winkle, you woke up one day and returned to the church. But you would never have expected anything like this! The altar is turned around, the Mass is in English, and who are all those regular people running around doing everything? Is it true that a married deacon has witnessed a marriage and a nun is editor of the diocesan newspaper? Is it true that people have to attend meetings before having their babies baptized? (I never had to do that!) Is it true that they baptize kids at Mass and anoint people there too? Is it true that they have something like a Methodist campfire meeting where everyone gets up and tells his or her sins? What *is* true is that the people in church are a noisy bunch before Mass. Where have the bells gone, the old sanctuary light, the tabernacle?

Yes, you remember fondly your childhood in the Catholic church: the beautiful, dark church with its awesome statues, the flickering candles, the red sanctuary light, the processions, the reverential hush, the sense of mystery, the Latin, the incense, the novenas, Saturday confessions, no meat on Friday, the cassocked pastor whose word was law. You ask yourself, what happened to it all?

If you are an under-50 returning Catholic (most likely), you remember the "old" church, grew up in the "new," but basically you too have the same question as your older counterpart: What happened to it all?

To both your questions of "What happened?" I respond, "Well, how far back do you want to go?" And I answer my own question by suggesting that you should go back to the beginning—or at least beyond your present experience of church, since what has happened has roots deep in the centuries. So as you strive to get reacquainted with your church and want a little background about where you are and where we all are in today's Catholic church, I invite you for a hop-skip-and-jump overview that might help put things in perspective before we tackle the specific issues.

A Mindset

As a member of today's generation you are probably imbued with the modern mindset that everything is relative. Television has shown us people of different cultures and different lands who come at life and live and die differently from us. The talk shows, from Donahue to Oprah, parade a startling array of different (and wild and kinky) lifestyles. And who's to say they're any better or worse than anyone else's? No doubt about it, through *National Geographic* and the mass media we know more "horizontally" than ever before. What goes on in Vietnam, Washington, Lebanon, or Tokyo is flashed immediately into our living rooms.

That mindset travels to the past "vertically" as well. All of a sudden we know much more about the past than ever before. What was thought to be the last word in one era—

for example, doctors putting leeches on people to draw out "bad blood"—is this era's nonsense.

We know more about the ancient world than the ancients themselves, for they had only pieces of the puzzle. We have the overview. We can see how things, people, attitudes, practices developed. We can distinguish more than ever before what is essential to a culture or a civilization—or a church—and what is minor and accidental.

A Dig Here, A Dig There

In 1993, the papers reported that scientists had discovered the outer walls of the fabled city of Troy. You might remember that Troy was a mythical city in Homer's *Odyssey*, and its chief inhabitant, Helen of Troy, had that face "that launched a thousand ships" to start the Trojan War. For centuries people continued to think that Troy was only a make-believe city in a make-believe story, the product of the poet's imagination. But not everyone. Some few believed it was a real city with a real history. They looked. They searched. They dug. Finally, in the 19th century a man named Heinrich Schliemann discovered it. And now, a century later, someone else has discovered its outer walls. And in that discovery, how much more about the ancient Greeks have we learned and will continue to learn!

There were other 18th- and 19th-century discoveries. Sir Arthur Evans discovered the palace of Minos on the isle of Crete. In Napoleon's time, one of the soldiers on an Egyptian desert campaign discovered the famous Rosetta Stone. No one could read it until a Frenchman named Champollion unlocked the hieroglyphics in the 1880s—and what a flood of new and intriguing information about one of the world's great civilizations burst forth! In the 1900s, ancient Babylonia began to be uncovered. Northeast of Baghdad an American expedition was discovering temples and palaces about which nothing heretofore had been

known. In 1971, a piece of Homer's *Odyssey*, going back to
the 3rd century, was discovered; this enabled scientists to
test the accuracy of the text we have today (remarkably accurate!).

The point is that all of these discoveries, and many more,
are comparatively recent. They've blown our minds and
have helped us enormously to understand the past and to
revise the present. And we're still discovering more every
day.

These discoveries have been made possible, of course, by
modern science. One simple example is the airplane. For the
first time in history people could fly *over* the land. And from
that vantage point they could see mounds that obviously
hid cities beneath them. Carbon count techniques can meas-
ure the time of an artifact within two hundred years and
closer. Echo chambers detect hidden cities or graves or palaces. Old manuscripts have been found. Sonar, x-rays, laser
beams, and a whole array of modern gadgets ferret out the
past.

Digging Up the Church
The Catholic church has been an intimate part of Western
civilization for two thousand years. (It has the longest consecutive existent government in the world: 2000 years. The
next longest is the United States Government: 200 years.) As
part of the past as well as the present, the church has a long
history and tons and tons of material, some of it hidden for
a long time and only comparatively recently found.

For instance: There's a very early Christian document
called *The Didache* (or "Teaching of the Twelve"). It likely
comes from the first half of the 2nd century. It was only discovered in 1875. You can imagine the wealth of information
there about the beginning church and how it made us take a
second look at what we were doing. The so-called Epistle to
Barnabas was found in 1859 in St. Catherine's monastery sit-

uated on Mt. Sinai. The systematic excavations of the Roman catacombs were only begun in the early 19th century under Pope Pius IX—and what inscriptions and graffiti there were, and how much they told us! Do you recall (if you're old enough) that the old *Life* magazine had those exciting pictures of St. Peter's grave with his bones in it found in the diggings under St. Peter's Basilica in Rome? No wonder they built the first church there on such an awkward site (on the side of a hill; they had to do a lot of fill work) rather than on the flat land nearby. Obviously the site was sacred and now we know why.

In 1945, a Gnostic library was found that has shed a lot of light on early church times. In 1961, the name of a man who was known only in the gospels and nowhere else was found inscribed on a pillar found in Caesarea in Palestine. The name: Pontius Pilate. In 1990, a Jerusalem bulldozer accidentally scraped off the roof of an ancient grave. Anthropologists were called in and after serious study proclaimed that this was the tomb of Caiaphas, the high priest at the trial of Jesus. We're still finding things!

Practical Fallouts

And we're all aware—for it's still very much in the news (intrigue, suppression, jealousy, etc.)—of the famous discovery in 1948 by a shepherd boy of the Dead Sea Scrolls. These scrolls are revealing much about the times just before and at the time of Jesus, an era heretofore little known or understood. They are the veritable remains of a library dating back to John the Baptist and Jesus. From these scrolls we learn that a group of people called the Essenes thought the Jewish Temple was corrupt and they left it for the caves of the desert. Reflections of this attitude are found also in the gospels.

Even more to the point: There are, as you know, four gospels. The first three, written in the 70s and 80s, Matthew,

Mark, and Luke, are so similar that the scholars recognize that they leaned in some way on one another.

But then there's that fourth gospel, the gospel of John. It's so different and so filled with Greek ideas and language that most scholars thought that it was a very late gospel, probably written around the year 150 or maybe a few years earlier, but not much. Being that late, it reflects another era far from the time of Jesus and can't possibly be very historical. But the Dead Sea Scrolls have shown us differently. They have shown us that the language and ideas of John's gospel were in fact quite current in the time of Christ. Furthermore, by comparing John's gospel to the Scrolls, it turns out that John's gospel, now dated more likely around the year 90, is far more historical than the other three.

Has that made a difference? Indeed. To share a very practical and sensitive application of this gospel's being closer to the scene and the facts of the passion of Jesus, we can now see that *John's gospel corrects the source of anti-Semitism found in the first three gospels.* In those gospels, a surface reading blames *all* of the Jews for the death of Christ (". . . the Jews who killed the Lord Jesus": thus St. Paul writing around the year 52 in the earliest New Testament writing; and "His blood be upon us and our children": Matthew 27:25), and this has snowballed throughout the centuries into violent anti-Semitism against the "God-killers."

But John's more accurate gospel shows that the blame falls on *only* the Roman officials in collaboration with *some* of the Jewish leaders—not all the Jewish people. And so Vatican II has corrected this anti-Semitism stance and changed and reworded the church's worship services that might have strengthened that wrong impression.

Churchy Perspectives
Let us pursue this historical look a little further. Since we've been rediscovering the past, no longer can the average

Catholic wrap himself or herself in their 40 or 50 years and declare of the church, "This is the way it's *always* been!" No. We just know too many things now. For example:

+ We know that the first pope and others after him did not wear the tiara or reside in the Vatican by St. Peter's in Rome. (They resided in Jerusalem, in Antioch, and in Avignon, France.) Popes have been there by St. Peter's (finished in the 16th century) only about 100 years. They had lived in the Roman Lateran Palace, and it was only around 1870 when Pius IX was fleeing the revolutionaries that he fled to the Vatican Hill and made himself a "voluntary prisoner of the Vatican." It's jarring, but it's possible that the pope could move to your town. But not fitting. It is better and more significant to be bishop of Rome where Peter and Paul laid down their lives.

+ We realize now that Masses were not celebrated either in churches or cathedrals for the first three hundred years, since during this time Christianity, which was prohibited, was an underground religion. The people gathered in "house churches" for their sharing of the word and the breaking of the Bread. In countries where religion is suppressed today, that's precisely what's happening.

+ We know that there were a variety of liturgies in the early centuries

+ that Communion under both species was the norm (and, later, when and why it was changed back to one species)

+ that women were active in the early church

+ that in the 7th century it was the practice of the Eastern Christians to communicate themselves

+ that the Blessed Sacrament was not reserved in church but in homes (and only to be used in case of dying, not for adoration)

+ that it was only in the 8th century that the little white round host replaced the regular bread at the Eucharist

+ that in the 11th century, incense, heretofore associated with pagan worship, was brought into the Christian church
+ that in the 11th century Pope Nicholas II invented the office, or rank, of Cardinal
+ that in the 14th century, Benediction, Forty Hours, and the Stations of the Cross were introduced
+ that the rosary itself is a product of the 15th century, and the Hail Mary did not receive its final form till the 16th century
+ that First Fridays did not appear till the 19th century
+ that first communion and first confession at the age of seven did not occur till the 20th century.

So?

What we have learned from this peek into history is that we can separate in our faith what is essential truth from what is accidental or a cultural (and lovely) expression of that truth. So, for example, Mary is essential to our faith. She is, as modern Scripture scholars have pointed out, the first and most faithful disciple of Jesus. The gospels increasingly point to her as a model of true discipleship and a woman of spiritual stature. And the ages have built on this and provided a cultural "trajectory" of honoring her. Sometimes through the years we have gone so far as to obscure her claim to fame as a disciple of *Jesus*, but for the most part we have tried to imitate her imitation of her Son. The rosary would be a gracious expression of devotion to this saint of reflected glory. But, of course, since it only came in the 15th century, that form of Marian devotion could hardly be essential for salvation. If it were, the Blessed Mother herself could not be saved, since she obviously did not say her own rosary!

The point is that such cultural expressions or variations can be freely altered, modified, or let go altogether because we have come to make the distinction between the essentials of our Christian faith and the styles and customs that enfold or express it.

Conclusion

The conclusion to this rapid survey is that you should be prepared for some changes—perhaps some of them jarring and drastic—as you come back home. For while you were gone, history has happened and facts have surfaced and some of the things we did and the ways we acted as Catholics for the past hundred years have been modified in the light of new discoveries of the past.

Therefore, all I wanted to do in this introductory chapter is make you aware that the changes you're encountering—some good, some bad; the agenda is still not finished—are not the result of some plot to overthrow the church or the mean-spirited revenge of the pope who stubbed his toe getting out of bed; but rather the changes are the result of a long process that was going on for about 150 years, a long process of discoveries, counterpointing (what we're doing now vs what they did then) and coordinating until all the scholarship, all the speculation, all the wide-eyed revelations burst forth in Vatican II.

I have in effect simply asked you to play the part of the old Roman god, Janus (after whom we name our first month). That's the god of gates and doors who had two faces so he could look backward and forward at the same time.

Resources

Gods, Graves and Scholars by C.M. Ceram (Random House, 1986). A paperback that reads like a detective novel and depicts the beginnings of archaeology.

The Churches the Apostles Left Behind by Raymond E. Brown (Paulist Press, 1984). A short book that gives us a survey of how the first churches survived after the death of the apostles.

Responses to 101 Questions on the Dead Sea Scrolls by Joseph Fitzmyer, S.J. (Paulist Press, 1992).

Chapter 2

WE AND THEE

"Those" People

The media being what it is, I am sure that you have heard some shocking things that this or that theologian is teaching. Some of them have had their official teaching licenses taken away. Names in the media are Charles Curran, Hans Küng, Matthew Fox, Leonardo Boff. But it's not just these people, but those anonymous "they" people that others keep telling you about—much to your bewilderment and perhaps exasperation. Hearing or reading about such "dissidents" in the church, you may be wondering what you came home to.

"They" say:

+ there is no such thing as original sin
+ there was no Magi following a star (the Magi are part of a made-up symbol story representing the Gentiles also receiving the Good News)
+ that Jesus was born in Nazareth, not Bethlehem (there go all those Christmas carols!)
+ you don't have to go to confession any more and besides

there's no such thing as mortal sin (When's the last time you heard the terms "mortal " and "venial " sin?)

+ that the pope isn't in charge
+ that eating meat on Fridays is all right
+ that women don't have to wear hats in church
+ that priests may get married
+ that women may be ordained
+ that birth control's all right, no matter what the pope says
+ that a nun in Alaska witnessed a marriage
+ that the *people* are the church, and priests may come and go, but this parish community remains
+ and who are these married deacons, anyway?

Frustration

And so it goes: a combination of real or imagined changes, the serious and trivial, rumor and fact—they have an unsettling effect. Where's that old monolithic church of my parents' time? There is a sinking sensation that everything one remembers from the past is now invalid or at least suspect. And the question arises, "If what I was taught in the past is all wrong, did my church lie to me? All those things I was taught as true without deviation, without hesitation, without qualification or explanation—they're not true any more?" I'm at bay and feel a little cheated, not to say confused as I make my way back to this infallible (?) church.

So, as part of your "re-education," let's explore two categories under the headings of "We" and "Thee." By "we" I mean anyone who has ever taught in the name of the church, any official or unofficial church teachers from the priest and sister to your CCD teacher, to the sermons you heard, the catechism you studied, to the lore and directions your parents or relatives passed on about the church. By "thee," or you, I mean you yourself and all those of your generation.

Unhistorical

Under the "we" category, let me state this truism. *In the past we taught unhistorically. Or, to put it another way, we taught religion without qualification.* One reason goes back to the first chapter. We just didn't know as much as we do today and so we simply passed on the current party line. In other words, we passed on what we were taught. Another reason was that, even if we knew there might be qualifications to what we taught, we were not encouraged to question or challenge, and so we did not allow you to do the same.

But another reason is that we had too much of a misdirected concern for our "spiritual children" who, we forgot, had grown up. Too many distinctions would confuse people, we rationalized. And, given the times, there was a good deal of truth in that stance. You see, you have no memory of our Catholic United States past.

Let me remind you that Catholics were very much unwelcomed in a land that was supposed to be a Protestant country. Crosses were burned in front of Catholics' houses. Catholics were not allowed to hold public office or vote at one time. (Remember, John F. Kennedy had a terrible time trying to prove he could be Catholic and president at the same time.) Priests were tarred and feathered. The Catholic immigrants who came over in waves at the turn of the century could not, except for the Irish, speak English. And they were not welcomed. They had no schooling, and many could not read or write. They had all they could do to earn a living, fight off prejudice, and get an education.

They sent for "their" priests from the other side. Soon there began a long, painful, and heroic climb to survival. Catholics clustered around their parishes, organized laborers to resist those who wanted to exploit them, established the Knights of Columbus (as a counter-organization to the hostile Masons), the CYO (as a counter-organization to the then hostile YMCA)—and, most gloriously and at great sacrifice, they put up their schools because the public schools were run by Protestants who insisted on the (Protestant) King James version of the Bible and often used anti-Catholic texts and examples. (Not: If you have four apples and take away three, what do you have? But: If you have four bad popes and take away three, what do you have?)

Well, when you're under attack like that, you tend to pull together and give one straight, defined position on everything. When you're under attack, there's no time for a lot of sophisticated speculation. Instead, we defended the people. Doctrine, like life itself, was direct. It made sense at the time to teach a preoccupied immigrant people in simple terms, direct quotations, and with firm authority. It was not a time for fine distinctions.

Not that distinctions, even in those days, were not there. They were. They always were. It was just felt that it was unnecessary and even dangerous to dwell on them at this time in our history. Besides, a strict party line was needed against those "others" (Protestants).

All right, never mind that for centuries there were other interesting theories on original sin or that some of the early Fathers spoke of several first parents. Never mind that St. Augustine (5th century) taught a Darwinian form of evolution. Never mind that the moral manuals listed an unusual amount of excuses for legitimately missing Mass. Never mind that a hundred years ago the Germans and French were rediscovering old liturgical books and were doing ancient liturgies in their monasteries. Never mind that the confessional box actually went back to the 16th-century Council of Trent (no, Joseph the carpenter did not build the first one.) Never mind that they used to give the sacred bread and wine to infants. All these things were true, but it was better to present one way, one theory, one custom as truth, rather than confuse the people who were just trying to get out of the sweat shops and ghettos.

Time Marches On

Well, time marches on. And you know what happened?
Two things: good news and bad news. The good news was
that in time the Catholic schools were spectacularly successful (even today, groaning under devastating financial burdens, the Catholic schools by all secular measurements are
superior to the public schools; and these days are educating
many poor minority groups). The Catholic schools did their
job. Catholics slowly got liberated and arrived where they
are today: fully educated and in the mainstream of life.

The bad news? "We" forgot to take notice. Now that we
could explore more with an educated people and open them
to our larger Catholic traditions, we didn't. Old habits die
hard and so, even though times had changed, we continued
to teach without qualification, giving only one (comparatively recent) view of Catholic doctrine and life or custom
where actually there were many. We indiscriminately
lumped together church homemade laws with the laws of
God. And we continued to censor scholars and new ideas.
The result of all this was to harden into a kind of absolute
dogma which was in reality either theory or one aspect of
the tradition. No multiculturalism here.

You can guess what happened. Predictably when the
now educated Catholics began to perceive *other* notable traditions in their church, when "subversive memories" from
the past began to surface, when Vatican II looked at the
practices of the past and the possibilities of the future, many
Catholics were caught off guard and it looked to them like
everything was up for grabs. And that's one reason you
might be puzzled at some teachings you hear in church or
from your child's religion teacher. And it's also why you
hear Catholics calling for (and fighting for) changes such as:

+ more involvement of women in ministry because they
   learned that women were active in the early and med-
   ieval church, so why not now?

+ allowing married priests because they now know that celibacy became a law only in the 12th century, and that Eastern priests were always allowed to be married
+ participation of the people and clergy in the election or choice of a bishop because they realize it's been done in the past—and the very recent past at that
+ less authoritarian style of leadership because they remember Jesus' words that the one who would be over you must be the servant of all.

These are old traditions and "we" could have helped make the transition smoother by surfacing them. Or by at least remembering that Catholics had in fact moved from being ignorant, ghettoed, uneducated immigrants to urban, college-degreed, world citizens. If only we had remembered that we did such a fantastic job in getting them from here to there. But in hindsight that was not as easy as it sounds for another reason: We had also inherited a very strong defensive posture that made it difficult to change.

The Defensive Posture

There's a second area of blame on the "we" side. *We taught from a background of fear and reaction.* To appreciate that, we must once more cast an eye on history. Note these profound items:

+ In the 14th century, the Bubonic plague (the "Black Death") wiped out one-fourth of the population of Europe. Today's AIDS infection is minor compared to that, but from the AIDS deaths we can catch a feeling for the deep sadness and despair that gripped the people. And why shouldn't people raise questions about God, suffering, and the purpose of life? The Black Death shook the church to its core as it tried to come up with answers.
+ In the 15th century, grave corruption in the Catholic

church undermined confidence in it as people cried for reform.

+ In the 16th century, reform did come in the form of the Protestant Reformation and in the rise of nationalism where the state would become more important than the church and indeed would become its rival (to this day). The church reacted defensively 20 years later with the Council of Trent, but by then all of Scandinavia, the British Isles, and much of Germany, Austria, and France had separated from the Catholic church. You can imagine what chaos went on and how badly the church had been wounded. This century surely marks the end of christendom and the beginning of modern Catholicism.

You can understand too why the Council of Trent reacted as it did. After all, what was at stake was the very authority of the church itself, and so the council came down heavily on that issue and strongly emphasized the external structure (not the internal life) of the church. The council wrapped the church in isolation and fashioned it into a kind of self-sufficient island kingdom untouched by the world. All kinds of self-protecting regulations were passed: the Index of Forbidden Books, rubrics standardizing the liturgy all over the world, and a single formulation of dogma (up to that time there were many legitimate formulations). It was the beginning of a static period only ending with the Second Vatican Council in our lifetime. Remember, your parents and teachers were brought up in this church.

The Council of Trent was held to present the authoritative answers of the Catholic church to the objections of the Protestant reformers. In order to promote Catholic unity, clear definitions were given concerning Catholic dogma. For example, a definition of the church's role emerged that stressed its visible institutional structures and identified the church with the kingdom of God on earth. Because of the narrowness of this definition, Catholicism tended to become exclusivistic in its thinking and static in its world view. The Council of Trent also issued a number of regulations to promote unity. As we have seen, the liturgy of the Mass was standardized and the *Index of Forbidden Books* was issued. These edicts helped maintain Catholic uniformity for the four hundred years after Trent. Great stress was placed on church authority to maintain this post-Tridentine Catholic oneness.

Robert A. Burns, *Roman Catholicism: Yesterday and Today*

+ In the 17th century, the Enlightenment extolled reason at the expense of faith and held sway to our day when its principles are seen to be bankrupt.

+ In the 17th century too, scientists like Galileo challenged the view of the world as taught by ordinary science of the day and the church; and when in due time he was proved right, the church was left with egg on its face and became defensive. (Galileo was officially exonerated by the church in 1992.)

+ In the 18th century, revolutions were in the air—the French and the American—which the church opposed. There indeed were terrible oppressions and blood baths, and the church was scared off and and wound up supporting kings and tyrants over democracy.

+ In the 19th century, the Industrial Revolution was born, dislocating families and breaking them up and loosening the church's hold on family life. Anti-Catholicism and anti-clericalism were rampant, causing a defensive posture.

+ In the early 20th century, there was a so-called heresy called Modernism which was trying to come to terms with new discoveries (such as we mentioned in the first chapter) and biblical and liturgical insights, but this frightened Rome and so it started a reign of terror by dismissing or suppresssing Catholic teachers, monitoring seminaries and newspapers, censoring books, and generally tightening control over all aspects of Catholic life. Authority, now firmly centralized in Rome (but only since the last century), was strongly vertical: from the pope on down to your local pastor and grade-school child.

The result of all these consecutive "body blows" in the last five centuries was to push the Catholic church off center stage, which it had occupied for so long, and understandably to make it very defensive. The church, once the patron of the arts and sciences, became suspicious of them. It invented the Index of Forbidden Books, scoffed at Darwin, made fun of Freud, condemned Margaret Sanger, separated from the Protestants, condoned anti-Semitism, and retreated into its own ghetto.

Again, we must remember that in many ways the church was under siege. The fortress mentality was forged from these past experiences. The church had to declare loud and clear: We have all the truth; others don't. We would be saved; others lost. Authority was strict, dialogue was out, and obedience in, and we saw to it that people would be kept safe from "dangerous" ideas. Even though many wonderful securities and benefits and a rich Catholic devotional life were evident, this ghetto mentality, this separation from the world, couldn't hold forever. It officially burst with Vatican II.

Anyway, the point of all this? "We" made mistakes in teaching so narrowly and defensively. Now, since Vatican II, we're trying to open up Catholics to our rich and varied Catholic past. We're making proper distinctions between what is a cultural expression (for example, Eastern Catholics bow and bless themselves right to left while Western

Catholics genuflect and bless themselves from left to right) and what is essential (we are saved by the cross of Christ, no matter how we make its sign). But, of course, that's why things are in a bit of confusion right now and why you, as a returning Catholic, might be disturbed over "new" teachings and emphases, why you might understandably hanker for those old "certainties." But the fact is that you—and all of us—have to live a while in the "in-between time" of ambiguity until we forge a new Catholic synthesis. So if, as a returning Catholic, you're confused at what you're hearing, welcome to the club!

The "You" Problem

We've confessed our sins. Now it's your turn. And here I have to challenge you. Let me put it this way. Think of your line of work. Do you really believe that you or anyone could function at your job if the last understanding and instruction you had was 20 years ago? Look around you at the technology explosion. People are using computers and if the kids are going to make it in the job market they better learn them early. Many jobs are now obsolete, done with new technology and marketing. Everything in your life right now has required some upgrading. Except religion.

People keep up with the latest fashion and celebrities, can recite the litany of Holywoood marriages, divorces, and face-lifts, can recount major league standings with remarkable accuracy, memorize fast rap lyrics, and give the names of the Teen Age Mutant Ninja Turtles. They are current on current affairs. Except religion.

You get my point. If you stopped formal religious education after confirmation or high school, you simply have to have wide gaps in your religious knowledge today. Think seriously: When was the last time you read a religious book or magazine or attended a lecture on a religious topic? Look in your magazine rack and note all the magazines you read and tally up the hours you watch TV—and you begin to realize that your input on religion is next to zero. You've kept up with a smattering of other things—but not religion. The bottom line is that if you've been pulling off a religious Rip Van Winkle stunt, you ought not to be surprised when you wake up to find a strange new (Catholic) world. In short, as you return you have some catching up to do. I hope this book will help.

Resources

Pilgrim Church by William J. Bausch (Twenty-Third Publications, 1989). A one-volume popular history of the Catholic church. See especially Chapter 24, "The Church in the United States."

A Concise History of the Catholic Church by Thomas Bokenkotter (Doubleday, 1979). Very good overview.

Roman Catholicism: Yesterday and Today by Robert A. Burns, O.P. (Loyola University Press, 1992). Good summary.

The Protestant Crusade by Ray Allen Billington, first published in 1939 and reprinted several times since. An old classic by a Protestant. An eye opener.

Once a Catholic by Peter Occhiogrosso (Houghton Mifflin, 1987). First-hand stories of what it was like to come to hostile America.

American Catholics by James Hennesey, S.J. (Oxford University Press, 1981). The best volume on our history.

Chapter 3

MEMORIES

Being Away

You have lots of company two ways. The first is that you've been away from the church and so have millions of others. The second is that you have returned and so have millions of others. You're among the Baby Boomers and Baby Busters who have come back. But the question is, why were you and the others away to begin with? That's what we're going to explore in this chapter. If the first two chapters tried to challenge your mind by looking at the context of what's happened in this old church of ours to cause so many changes, this chapter seeks to challenge your heart by looking at the alienation and hurts that made you leave or drift away in the first place.

First, let's see who you (likely) are. You are the Baby Boomers, the 76 million people born between 1946 and 1964 and the most educated (and often affluent) group in United States history (60 percent attended college). This means that you are either a product of the fabled Sixties (early liberal Baby Boomers, that is, from 1946 to 1954; for example, Bill Clinton, Al Gore, and practically all of their cabinet) or

products of the experimental Seventies (the late, more conservative Baby Boomers born between 1955 and 1962). All
this in turn means you have memories. Those in their 40s remember a time of great upheavals, the drug culture, the sexual revolution, peace movements, civil rights, expectations,
and hope. Those younger remember the evangelical and
charismatic revivals of the Seventies, the greed and New
Age spiritualities of the Eighties.

And all, directly or indirectly, remember disillusionment:
Vietnam, protests, the assassinations of John F. Kennedy,
Martin Luther King, and Bobby Kennedy, and later,
Watergate, environmental pollution, and family breakdown.
All are heirs to the women's movement, high lifestyle tolerance, the primacy of choice (how *you* feel has replaced outside authority, including God), and television, which has
replaced pretty much the authority of parents and given
you a world in which the written word is far less important
than the image.

At the same time, it means that you are also heirs to the
breakdown of authority and the family. (You have a good
chance statistically of being a child of divorce yourself.)
Four out of every ten children today are born out of wedlock. The epidemic of crime has become so commonplace
that, as Sen. Daniel Moynihan of New York has pointed out,
it has become normalized. (In 1993, for example, New York
City spent 73 million dollars on security in its public schools
for guards and metal detectors. Baltimore had 365 murders
in one year, one for each day. Washington, D.C., is called
the murder capital of the world.) Then there is the pervasive
drug problem, AIDS, and all the rest of the fears and anx-
ieties that form the content of our nightly newscasts.

Such is the context of your lives. The result of these upheavals is to bequeath to many of you (not all, but enough
to make some generalizations) a strong sense of tolerance,
self-reliance, and self-improvement, and, that strongest of

characteristics, self-fulfillment. You take multiple options for granted and completely believe in gender equality in home and at the workplace. Bred in the affluent post-war years, you have a sense that you're entitled to the good things in life and, honed with such ongoing and persistent changes in your life, you have a very strong resistance to making "final choices" about anything. You likely harbor a firm distrust of all institutions: political parties, government, the military, big business, schools—and organized religion.

And speaking of organized religion, you have memories here too. One memory is that you left it. That would put you among the two-thirds of the Boomers who do. That raises the question, why did *you* leave and why do people in general leave in the first place? Besides the normal lifecycle departures for the 18 to 28 group (we will mention them below) who have drifted into being inactive Catholics, there are those of any age who have simply left the church. They made a decision to drop out. Why? You can't answer for them, but you can stir up your own memories. Just as you have memories of society in the Sixties or Seventies so you have memories of the Catholic church when you were growing up. What are they? They're worth recalling for, in reality, they may still be very much functioning.

The Dysfunctional Catholic Family

The words dysfunctional and co-dependent originally were used to describe the families of alcoholics, but they've gone beyond that. They're used today pretty much to express people's thoughts and feelings and actions generated by a negative self-definition. In other words, we've all been affected for better or for worse by the past. For some people the strongest memories are those of their Catholic past, again, for better or for worse. For some, their positive self-definition was either given by the home or enhanced by their experience of the church. Many people have great

memories of growing up Catholic and the popularity of the
play *Nunsense,* for example, now running for some eight or
nine years, still convulses Catholic audiences who resonate
with the old symbols, rituals, and habits (the dress) of the
nuns and priests. As one middle-aged Boomer recollects:

> After 25 years, I can still remember the cataclysmic
> events of 1968—from the assassinations of Robert
> Kennedy and Martin Luther King to the Apollo 8 mis-
> sion and the nightly newscasts of fighting in Vietnam.
> The world looked different after 1968; things were nev-
> er the same. . . .
>
> Under the watchful eye of the Marist Brothers, I
> came of age discussing the grave moral issues of our
> time which included everything from necking to draft-
> dodging. In a society undergoing radical changes, the
> Marists had clear priorities and they made sure we
> shared them. . . . After 25 years I realize St. Joseph's of-
> fered me a point of reference in a chaotic society that
> was changing irrevocably. It offered stability at a time
> when there was little stability in the world.
>
> J.F. Pisani *(Our Sunday Visitor,* April 11, 1993)

Many Catholics, in spite of so much negative press from
those disaffected, have fond memories of the church.
They're grateful for it and love it dearly.

But, of course, there is an "on the other hand." Some
Catholics' negative self-definition often was either given or
aggravated. These are the people wearing the T-shirts, "I
Survived the Catholic Church." We don't mean the negative
self-definitions which are the result of the graver crimes,
such as being molested by a pedophile priest. Rather, I refer
to the teachings, attitudes, and hurts that people may have
received at the hands of the church. Some people's memories are sad. They carry around so much anger, for ex-

ample, because they were taught as seven year olds that Protestants weren't going to heaven, and one of their parents was Methodist. Or if they touched the sacred Host with their fingers when it stuck to the roof of their mouths they would commit a mortal sin. Or they were told they were unworthy, that God really didn't love them, that they were sinners and would wind up in hell. Or a sister cuffed them on the ear in the third grade or the priest yelled at them on the altar or in the confessional. Or the priests were always asking for money. Or they rejected your sister who was married and divorced.

Others move beyond the personal hurts and cite the church's rigidity: rules, rules, rules, and you never bend them. Others are disgusted with the church's inhumane actions (denying marriage to an AIDS victim) or failures (protecting priests who molest children while ignoring the victims) or neglect (not paying its employees a just wage). They are put off, to put it mildly, by the local pastor or nun or church minister who acts like a little pope by being harsh and unbending. They hate those authoritarian representatives of the church who are supposed to represent a loving God and God's mysterious and pervasive love and box it into rigid rules and regulations.

Sexuality

Then there's the big ones, the really big ones: Many disagree with the church's stand on sexuality, from masturbation and premarital sex to abortion. The common popular concept is that in the eyes of the church there is sin and there is *the* sin: sex. There's so much hypocrisy going around in their eyes. They read with cynicism the sexual failures of priests and bishops who break their vows and have sexual relationships. There's a credibility issue here. And what about the birth control issue? Surveys show that Catholics use birth control in the same proportion as everyone else, and

that 80 percent of them think it's morally all right and disagree strongly with the church's official stance of prohibition. Who wants to stick with a church that's so far off
the mark?

Others are involved in divorce and remarriage and they
simply don't know where they stand in the church and they
are aggrieved that they can't receive the Eucharist. They feel
anger, pain, isolation, and shame. They hear all kinds of
misinformation about annulments: how long it takes, how
intimate the information sought, how much money it costs.
Then there's the gay and lesbian Catholics who are sad-
dened over the church's stance.

There's also the progressive Catholics who left because
the spirit of Vatican II in their eyes has been betrayed. They
have a lot of anger. Or the conservative Catholics who feel
the church has sold out to the progressives. There's the anger of women over the official prohibition of altar girls (perhaps at last soon to be changed), not to mention ordination
for women and in general the low status of women in the
church. Some are distressed that church is so boring and the
preaching atrocious. Others have a lot of left-over guilt.
Others are distressed at the hierarchy. The list is long.

Perspective

But, as we said, many have returned. You have returned.
The facts show that people from the ages 18 to 28 fall away
from the church at a net rate of about one percent per year.
Low levels of devotion among such young adults are no
surprise and are correctly credited to rebellion (first time
away from home; you're on your own), isolation (not a family or neighborhood or friends who form a support group
that goes to church), experimentation (dipping into the New
Age practices), and other competing interests (Who has time
for church when you're having fun?). *But* after age 28, those
who leave are outnumbered by those who return. If you use

Mass attendance as a measurement, about 320,000 Catholics return each year. Returning Catholics like yourself are quite visible today. And even among those who have not returned, surveys show that 39 percent of them have thought about it. They just haven't gotten around to it.

Why do they return? You can supply your own answer for your return, but studies have given the following general reasons: 1) people feel a spiritual void in their lives; 2) some feel guilty about being away from the sacraments; and 3) since some are now in their 40s—"the old age of youth and the youth of old age"—they are facing a mid-life crisis about the meaning of their lives and, most of all, they are considering what they want for their children: They want them to have spiritual values in a world falling apart. 4) At this time, when the "Age of Greed" is over, people feel they want to commit themselves to something important, to connect to deeper relationships that will last. In short, they want something more stable in their lives.

You may have read your reasons here. Whatever they are, you have returned. Perhaps you are merely in your post-28 time frame; or if the reasons for your return are deeper than that, note this caution: You should be aware of your hurt or previous alienation and anger. You are likely still carrying them around with you buried inside you somewhere, and they are going to inhibit your full and joyous life in the church unless you come to terms with them. You should also be aware that there are ways of dealing with your alienation and anger. One direct and simple way is to realize that, in fact, in many ways (alas, not in all) things have changed.

Many parishes (I hope yours is one of them) are open and welcoming; they have Homecoming and Re-Membering programs offering opportunities for people like yourself to ventilate and lay their hurts to rest. Some offer small groups that would provide an opportunity for discussion and growth. Others have forums for people to talk through their alienation, a chance to tell one's personal story. Some offer gentle advice and services in relation to divorced and re-married couples. Some offer communal penance services that help reconcile guilt and sin.

Many returning Catholics are amazed to find how fully and completely women are now an active part of the church at the diocesan and parish levels. Many, as we shall see, are amazed to see how full the shared and collaborative ministries of clergy and laity are in the parish. In a word, I hope your parish experience shows you that things *have* changed and gives you the opportunity for emotional and spiritual growth when you reenter.

Recovery

But let's get back to the terms "dysfunction" and "co-dependent." The people who found religion flawed and left the church or even threw out God have come back but *still* walk around with a poor self-image and are still angry with the church, which keeps them constricted and unhappy. They are co-dependent because they are locked into their anger and are not really free.

If you're one of those who have painful memories about the church, you don't have to be a victim of the past. You have a choice: You can spend your life in resentment at some priest or sister who died 30 years ago, but, if you do, you have to ask yourself: Who's paying for that? You are. Or, you can realize that such experiences do not have to be an obstacle between you and God and your full return to the church. You can be freed of that negative past by becoming aware that you may need guidance and help to recover. As one psychotherapist says:

It is important to remember that the church (like a parent) is accountable for some of our present distress but is not responsible for it. To be accountable means to have played a part in the formation of a fear or a deficiency. To be responsible means to have caused it, i.e., to be the blame. The church is not causing nor has it caused our feelings. As adults, our work is to recognize our pain and to work with it for change. To hold onto it is a choice against change and growth and for such a choice we are the ones responsible. The work of recovery can never truly proceed as long as the church (or anyone else) is to blame, because we then become passive victims, unable to help ourselves. Only able (though wounded) adults can do this work for themselves on themselves.

David Richio (*The Catholic World*, March-April 1993)

That's easier said than done, but the point here is that it must be done if you are to return to your full heritage in the church. This is not the place to explain recovery but I can quickly pass along one writer's suggestions. Such recovery, he says, occurs on three levels: the mental, behavioral, and the level of accountability. On the mental level you must repeat affirmations—like little short prayers—every day on what you want to change; for example, "I am happy and healthy. God loves me." On the behavioral level, do one positive thing daily. For example, if I'm afraid of talking about my feelings, I might commit to sharing a feeling with my spouse every day. As for accountability, you need to have people (such as a prayer group) to whom you are accountable for continuing those affirmations and actions.

The point is that you have come back home. "Home," I trust, has improved a lot and you should enjoy being back. The riches of your heritage are here for you, You shouldn't be put off because of negative inner feelings from the past. You can take charge and find that life that Jesus claimed to give and to give abundantly.

Conclusion

In these first three chapters, I tried to give you, a returning Catholic, some context to your religious life and to the life of the church we call Catholic. You're a 20th-century person caught in the rapid changes of society. You're the end product of the severe dislocations of the last five centuries, the child of "future shock." You're experiencing a breakdown of the center of things. You're a Catholic of this time and place with all of the Catholic baggage—good and bad, great and ignoble—from the past. But by the grace of God, you have returned to your heritage. You have sought community in the Lord and hope to find meaning in your life *and* contribute to making things better.

Of course, you have some questions, some sense of unfamiliarity. The point of this chapter was simply to remind you of some background, some context in history—and in yourself—before you seek answers to what happened while you were gone.

Resources

Everybody Has a Guardian Angel by Mitch Finley (Crossroad, 1993). A recollection of growing up Catholic. Charming, inspirational, and timely. Get this one.

Recovering Catholics: What to Do When Religion Comes Between You & God by Earnie Larsen and Janee Parnegg (HarperSanFrancisco, 1992). Just what it says.

The Road Home: Five True Stories of Catholics Who Have Returned to the Church (Liguori Publications, 1985). You might want to read of others' journeys and recoveries.

Returning: A Spiritual Journey by Dan Wakefield (Doubleday, 1988). The story of a screenwriter-novelist's return to faith.

How to Reach Baby Boomers by William Easum, ed. Herb Miller (Abingdon Press, 1991). To give to your pastor or parish council.

Part Two

The Changes

Chapter 4

SUNDAY CONFUSIONS

Sacred Architecture
The church in which I worship is in the round with a free-floating altar in the free-standing sanctuary with no altar rail or other hindrance. It seats about 500 people and no one is more than ten pews from the altar. You can see everybody with ease and they can see you. The baptism font is up front right in the middle aisle. The tabernacle is off on a platform to the side, not on the altar. The church is bright with large stained-glass windows and a skylight; it also has a cry room. The sacristy is in the back. The Mass is in English with the priest facing the congregation. There are all kinds of people doing things: readers or lectors, Eucharistic ministers giving out communion, boy and girl acolytes, people saying petitions aloud. Almost everyone gets up and goes to Communion. There is some socializing before and after Mass. People are quite chatty. That's not the way I actually remember it; that's not the church of my childhood.

My childhood church—I remember it fondly—was rectangular with a long middle aisle. It was somewhat dark but this only enhanced the glow of the red sanctuary lamp that hung on a long chain from the high ceiling. The atmosphere was reverent. You hushed as you entered. The altar was against the front wall with the tabernacle on it flanked by a canopy of carved angels. The sacristy was a room behind the altar. The Mass was in Latin, with altar boys responding. The people were quiet; some said the rosary, read devotional prayers, or used missals with translations and pictures to see what part of the Mass the priest was at. The priest was alone and did the readings and distributed Communion to people kneeling at the altar rail. Most people did not go to Communion. Women wore hats. People came silently before Mass and stayed afterwards to pray. Then they genuflected and left.

Perhaps that's how you remember it. Or, more likely, you have never known the church and Mass of my childhood and your parents'. You were raised on the style of worship after Vatican II. What happened between my lifetime and yours? What puzzles you as you return to a vastly different church worship from your parents' time?

The Latest Mass

You have probably caught the notion by now that nothing stays static, and in the long course of 2000 years Christian worship has changed as you might expect it to. Let's start with the word "Mass." That name appeared only in the 4th century and slipped into popular use in the 5th and 6th centuries. Up to then it was known as "The Lord's Supper" because, in fact, that's where it all began. And, from the beginning, as you would expect in an oral culture, there was a variety of traditions and rituals for the different congregations of early Christians. We see this reflected in the variations found in St. Paul's epistles and in Matthew, Mark, and Luke's gospels.

To simplify things, we might say there are four phases in the development of the Mass. In the first centuries we have *the simple and flexible Mass*, say, from the 1st to the 4th centuries. The first Christians, being Jews, first went to the temple and then back to their homes for the "breaking of the bread," which they held during regular meal time. Since this breaking was perceived as a sacrifice, they soon began to separate from the temple and also eventually began to separate this breaking of the bread from their regular meals.

Likewise, being trained in Jewish ritual prayer, the first Christians added prayers and Scripture to their worship, especially after they were barred from the synagogue. And here you have the basic outline of our Mass to this day: the Word of Scripture and the breaking of the Bread. (These two parts were once known as the Mass of the Catechumens—which included the reading of Scripture and sermon, after which the catechumens, those being prepared for formal entry into the church, were dismissed—and the Mass of the Faithful, which was for the baptized, who could stay for the Eucharist.)

The bread they used was from the ordinary loaves baked and brought by the faithful as well as the unleavened bread used in Jewish Passover. And quickly the language changed, from the original Aramaic that Jesus spoke, to Greek, because that's what most of the new converts spoke. Later, when Greek fell into disuse, Latin was adopted (not without a fight!). Remember, all this was taking place in homes—and sometimes in catacombs—since Christianity was illegal. People stood around the table, which was the "altar," and received Communion standing. The prayers and wording of Mass differed from place to place. The people wore their everyday clothing at these celebrations.

The second phase is from the 4th to the 6th centuries and might be characterized as the *long and complicated Mass*. Christianity was now legal. Old grand temples were taken over and new basilicas built. The altar was still a simple table and the priest was still facing the people, but everything was longer, grander, and more solemn. Prayers for the living and the dead were added, as were ceremonies borrowed from the court ceremonial such as bowing, genuflections, kissing, using candles and incense, which were looked on with suspicion in an earlier age! The cult of the saints and martyrs became prominent.

Even though a pope, Celestine I, wrote in the 5th century that "we should distinguish ourselves from the people by doctrine, not by vestment . . ." eventually the garments worn at Mass were not worn at other times, and when styles changed, those clothes remained and we got the special liturgical vestments we have today.

As the small Christian groups became crowds, there was the need for more order and precision—a Roman specialty (think of the famous Roman law). The process and order of the Mass were written down and eventually the flexible prayers and ritual became standardized. There were many such standard books from the Christian world—from the areas we now call Germany and France, but the Roman rule (or canon) won out. St. Ambrose who lived in the 5th century reminded the people to answer "Amen" when they received Communion. Private Masses—Masses celebrated by the priest all alone with no one present—began to make their appearance in the monasteries, thus breaking down any and all communal aspects of worship. And, of course, Mass eventually became silent because the priest couldn't disturb all the other priests who were also celebrating Mass by themselves.

Reaction Time

The third phase is the *far away and silent era* of the 9th and 10th centuries. This is the Mass of your parents. What happened was that a couple of harsh heresies denied the divinity of Jesus, so in reaction the church came down hard on that side. In the process, Jesus' humanity was neglected. The simple and kindly Good Shepherd found in pictures in early baptistries gave way to the mighty and awesome Christ looking for all the world like a Byzantine emperor or Greek god. (For a good example of this, see the mosaic of Christ above the main altar in the National Shrine in Washington, D.C. It's not a picture to warm your heart.)

Anyway, to stress Jesus' divinity the Nicene creed was added to the Mass as well as prayers to the Trinity. Distance and unworthiness became the norm. If formerly the Mass was a gathering of the baptized around the altar with the bishop, now it became an occasion of separation. People began to feel overawed and unworthy of such a Divine Presence. Many confessions before Mass were introduced (the confiteor; Lord, have mercy). An altar rail now emphasized the distance. There was a preoccupation with cleanliness (all those white cloths), reverence (no talking in church, your Father's house!), remoteness (stay behind the rail). Absolutions and washings were introduced. Communion in the (dirty) hand was stopped. The bread became the small, white host (which we used to call irreverently the Necco wafer), hardly recognizable as bread. People were no longer worthy—and said so three times.

Since people had forgotten Latin, specialists were called in: altar boys and choirs. They did the speaking and singing parts. The now separated sanctuary was decorated and the priest wound up facing that decoration when they pushed the altar table back to the wall. The priest eventually took over all parts. People became spectators. The Mass prayers became a whisper, a concern only of the priest. At this time, too, the chalice was withdrawn from the people.

The fourth and final phase of the Mass's development till Vatican II can be labeled the *Mass of the rubrics*. Many abuses had sprung up and in reaction the Council of Trent issued decrees regulating every single word and action. Such directions were written in red—hence rubric (Latin, for red). This council froze the Mass into a precise ritual passively watched by the people who said their private prayers in the pews. Reaction to heresies and the Protestant reformers led the church to emphasize the presence of Christ in the Eucharist. Corpus Christi processions were introduced, Benediction, and finally, in the 17th century, tabernacles were ordered placed on every altar. The church in effect became a throne room for the Divine Christ with all the protocol of guards (Knights of Columbus), perpetual adorers, and sacred canopies. It was a far cry from the communal and simple meal of the Last Supper with a sorrowful Jesus sharing his words, wisdom, and very self in the breaking of the bread and sharing of the cup.

Today

That was a quick, much condensed summary, but you simply have to appreciate what has happened in the past to sense what happens in the present when you come to church to celebrate the Mass promulgated in 1970, the Mass of Vatican II. For one thing, like my church, yours may be designed not for remoteness and distance, not for private quiet time, but for community. Some churches have what they call a Gathering Space so people can socialize before and after Mass. It's certainly more untidy and noisy, and you can understand why some people complain about it. After all, they came to church to pray and don't want to be distracted.

The only problem with this view is that it's like going to a football game to read your novel and complaining about all the noise and distractions. A football stadium is *designed* for community, for communal activity, for the mob. If you want to read your book, go to your room or a library or a monastery. People who come to the parish church for quiet and solitude should come during the off-times when no one is there, not at high community-gathering time when people have come to worship precisely as a people, as a faith community.

But you can see what is happening. People with this view are still in the old church which was a haven, a throne room, a holy of holies, an inner sanctum. They look for darkness, silence, privacy, and are hurt or disappointed in not finding them. But a parish church on a Sunday is no place to seek solitude any more than going to the ball game that afternoon is. So if your first impression on returning is to notice the untidiness, that makes sense: You've come to a community event.

There's no altar rail because *all* the people are worshipping and praying with the celebrant; it's not the priest's Mass. There should be no division and separation any more than there were at the Last Supper or in the house churches of the first centuries. Worship belongs to the people. It's the People of God's community event, as we said, and it's only right that members of the congregation be active, not passive. That's why you'll find them reading (proclaiming) the Scripture, bringing up the gifts, distributing Communion, greeting the people, ushering for good order, cantoring, baking the bread, putting out the flowers, and assisting at the altar. "Pray, brothers and sisters, that my sacrifice and *yours* may be acceptable to God the Father Almighty." That's an old, old prayer now come to reality.

The far-away and silent Mass of the priest has given way to the near and vocal Mass of all the people. The altar rail is gone, the language returned, the priest once more faces the people as around the ancient table, and the tabernacle is off to the side or in a nearby chapel. Not because it is now unimportant, but because the lovely devotions to the Blessed Sacrament are private devotions for private times. On Sundays we've come to sit around the table and that table, or altar, is the focal point, where we will break bread together. We don't want to be distracted from that even by the tabernacle that houses our blessed Lord. (The Blessed Sacrament was never kept in church in early times, but in the rectory or elsewhere, and it was kept, not for adoration, but for one basic reason: to be given in an emergency to someone who was dying.)

Conclusion

The liturgy—to use the "in" term for communal worship—has changed from age to age. Some wonderful things have been lost, some found. People feel that the sense of mystery has disappeared in too much liturgical "democracy," that transcendence has been flattened out to the congregation, and the music has not even begun to catch up with the majesties of Gregorian Chant. There's some validity to these comments.

But the truth is that we're not through yet changing things. And the truth is also that much has been gained: a deeper sense of community, a richer sharing of gifts and talents, a sense of responsibility, an appreciation of local expression and culture. But above all the pros and cons, the reality remains: Jesus and his givingness and love demonstrated by a "Body given for you and a Blood shed for you." We must be sharers and participators in such mysteries, not passive bystanders. That's the reason for a return to the ancient ways, a return that challenges us all to lift up our hearts and to give thanks *together* to the Lord our God.

Resources

The Story of the Mass by Pierre Loret (Liguori Publications, 1982).

This Is Our Mass by Tom Coyle (Twenty-Third Publications, 1989). A fine, clear, simple description.

Chapter 5

SESSIONS AND SACRAMENTS

Alarm

If you're a parent or about to be one, you read in the parish Sunday bulletin or you received a letter in the mail the notice that you must attend classes, classes for all sorts of churchy things: classes for baptism, classes for your child's first communion, first penance, or confirmation. If you're single and are about to be married, you must attend pre-Cana classes. To do anything in the Catholic church it seems, you've got to go to some meeting or class. You begin to feel like the church has taken over the Politically Correct brainwashing classes of the universities. Your parents, or at least certainly your grandparents, didn't have to go to "classes" to get you baptized. You're beginning to get that feeling that the rules haven't lessened; they've multiplied.

As a returned Catholic, you want to know what's behind it all and how flexible these demands are. In a nutshell, the problem is that we're not sure we're talking the same language, so we have to meet to be sure we are. This is a variation on what was said in Chapter 2: We really don't know who's been away and who hasn't, and therefore who knows the latest insight and who doesn't. So we have no choice but to get together. Since any lack of common understanding will be most obvious in dealing with the sacraments, let's take a quick look at them to see if we both understand the same thing about them, or if, in fact, while you were gone, a lot has changed.

Baptism

You may think you know what baptism is all about. Your child has to get original sin off her soul so she won't go to limbo or hell, and you want her officially and certifiably "Catholic." Period. So what are you doing at pre-baptism classes? Your concepts are all right as far as they go, but they don't go far enough.

To begin with, we now have an excellent idea of how baptism began and what it was all about, and we've changed accordingly. Baptism, as we know now, was a single rite of entrance into the church that had three elements to it: the water, the anointing with oil, and the Eucharist. Initially only adults were baptized after a long, long period of preparation (prayer, charity, scrutiny, study, etc.). But due to historical pressures, the three movements were split off like the three movements of the one concerto. One—the anointing with oil—spun off into what was to be called confirmation, given many years after the pouring of the water, and the other—receiving the Eucharist—was moved from infancy to seven or so years later. Each got its own identity as separate sacraments when, in fact, they all belong together.

Today, we're trying to get the three movements, or sacraments, back together. That's why when we celebrate one sacrament we always do something to recall the other two. So, baptisms are routinely celebrated at Mass (Eucharist) and babies are anointed ("confirmation"). First communion? Children dip their hands in the baptism font as part of their ceremony (baptism). Confirmation is celebrated at Mass (Eucharist) and these young people also dip their hands in the font and bless themselves (baptism).

The baptism of infants evolved for a most practical and common-sense reason. In early times there was a natural community spirit. Parents set the tone for the children since the family was all one unit. If the parents were Christian, then it was assumed that the children would be. It would be as natural for them to be Christian as it would be for them to speak Greek or Latin. It was inconceivable that the faith, like language, would not be unconsciously passed along. The early Christians were *households of faith*. They could never imagine either the children being different from the parents or the culture not supporting both. And for many centuries the culture did. Christianity was "in the air."

Everywhere you went there were cathedrals with their carved figures telling the Bible story. There were holy days (not holidays), religious art, guilds named after saints, and outdoor shrines everywhere. You can still see remnants of these in Europe today. The culture was Christian. Parents had many "visual aids" and help in passing on the faith. To baptize infants in this climate made sense. One could assume a faith culture and one could assume faith-filled parents. But no more. Hence, pre-baptism classes to check out assumptions.

The Community Factor

Another insight of great practical importance is that baptism is basically the sacrament of initiation into a community, not primarily the sacrament of personal stain removal (original sin). Baptism is the life-long and committed rite of belonging, of freely accepting a way of life, of being inserted into the church through this particular parish or faith community. Therefore baptism is not a private, personal act (as your parents may have experienced in those baptisms on a Sunday afternoon in an empty church), but a public act, a public declaration that you have freely chosen for your child this way of life, this church, this tradition. Yes, there's the taking away of original sin but that's not the main focus. The main focus is committing one's child to Jesus and his community called the church. He or she is to walk with us, be part of our lives, mutual sharing of sorrows and joys. In short, the child joins the journey of us saints and sinners. We're bonded to each other. Baptism is a social contract.

Necessarily there is a deep and serious social responsibility that goes along with all this. That's why *you* are challenged—gently, I hope—at the pre-baptism meeting. Because, when you come right down to it, any parents who request baptism for their child are making a profound decision for *themselves*. Are they ready to live the faith? Are they ready to accept the old truism that religion is not taught but caught: caught from the parents' fidelity to church, prayer, and good works?

If not, if there is unfaithfulness on the part of the parents, you may sometimes hear of baptisms being delayed, at least till further dialogue can be had coaxing the parents to live what they want their children to be by having them baptized. So, you may be thinking inoculation against original sin, but we're thinking community. You may be thinking of stamping your child Catholic, but we're thinking journey: It's going to take a lifetime to grow into being a full Christian. You may be thinking private ceremony, but we're thinking public acceptance, welcome, and commitment. *That's* what's changed while you were gone.

Confirmation and Anointing of the Sick
Since, as we noted above, confirmation is really a part of baptism initiation, then this sacrament has all the markings of being a further step in the process of becoming Christian.

The young people speak for themselves in affirming their parents' choice and, since being a Christian is to do the works of the gospel, there is always a service requirement for the candidates for confirmation (such as accounting for 15 hours of service: at a nursing home, babysitting for free, etc.). You may remember the slap on the cheek the bishop gave at confirmation (we had great fun imagining a mighty blow that would send us reeling down the aisle). No more. That "blow" was an evolved kiss of peace as one would touch another gently to show affection. Today the bishop skips the slap and simply says, "Peace be with you."

The old extreme unction has had a name change. That's because for too long we had thought erroneously that the word extreme meant last: You were on your way out. Yes, it means last, but only in the sense that this anointing is normally the last in the series of anointings that go from baptism to confirmation to holy orders. So the name has been changed to "sacrament of the sick" because this anointing was *not* meant to speed people off to eternity or to grease those already dead into heaven. Rather, it traditionally was meant to assist the living sick and even to heal them. Life is the emphasis, not death.

So this sacrament has nothing to do with the "last rites" in the sense of finality and therefore has nothing to do with anointing a dead person. It has everything to do with those mentally, emotionally, and physically ill who need the ministrations of the church and the prayers of the all the People of God now. Which is why if such an anointing is done at home or hospital or nursing home, everyone is invited to be there and take part. It's a community event. And all the more reason why often such anointings are done at Mass before the entire community.

Of course, those who don't know this shift are angry that the priest would not give the "last rites " to Grandpa who's been dead three hours. (But surely the priest comes and says the lovely prayers of commending the deceased to God.) Or there are still those who will not call the priest for sick grandma since his very presence is likened to a visit from the Grim Reaper and sick grandma will suspect something's up. So this sacrament is not the last rites for dead, or almost dead, people. It's a sacrament for people who are alive, but ill. That's what's changed while you were gone.

Confession and Matrimony

Confession's had a name change too, to underscore a better emphasis. Confession put the emphasis on an impersonal "grocery list" of sins and all the mathematics and mechanics involved with number, kind, and circumstance. But the new name underscores the personal aspect. This sacrament is now called the "sacrament of reconciliation." You can have reconciliation only between two people, so the word conjures up, as it is meant to do, the Father embracing his returned Prodigal Son. Likewise, to emphasize the personal, people have an option of reconciling in a confession room, sitting down face to face with the priest.

We also emphasize the community ramifications of sin for, after all, sin may be secret, but all sin is communal; it affects the community. The virtues or vices of the individual raise or lower the general sanctity of us all, just as the honesty or theft of one student raises or lowers the trust level of the whole classroom. So we have communal confessions where the entire congregation meets with an understanding that we are mutually responsible for one another and that our moral lives impinge on each other. Thus we gather in solemn prayer, Scripture, examination of conscience, reconciliation, and thanksgiving. Sometimes there are many priests to hear individual confessions at these gatherings; or if there is a very large crowd and few priests, general absolution is given. Such a ceremony is worth attending. A deeper sense of the personal and a deeper sense of the social impact of sin: That's what's changed while you were gone. As for matrimony, well, we don't need too much conviction to see that some preparation is in order, and the wisdom of giving the parish at least eight months notice, and why the couple should attend pre-Cana classes. Once we could assume a stable couple from a stable neighborhood from stable parents. No more. Family life is under terrible siege. Broken homes, out of wedlock birth, abortions, live-in companions, a recessive economy have had a huge negative impact on children. One out of five children lives below the poverty line. Four out of every ten children born today are born out of wedlock. Almost half the marriages end in divorce. In this climate you can see that the engaged couple need to be challenged (and helped) as to their own background, expectations, and promise of fidelity and permanency.

But, aside from these matters, many externals concerning the wedding ceremony have changed. For instance, a Catholic may marry a non-Catholic at a Nuptial Mass; a wide range of acceptable music is available; the ceremony may be quite personalized; family and friends may take part in the liturgy. It's a warmer, friendlier, community affair.

Funerals

The Mass of the Dead has given way to the Mass of Christian Burial. Vestments have gone from black to white. The phrase "Christian burial" sounds a note of hope and the white vestments harken to the reality of the resurrection. Grief and sorrow are still very much a part of a funeral, as indeed they should be, but the undercurrent of belief in the resurrected Christ who gives life is attested to. Many parishes (like our own) have wakes in church. All encourage personal participation: Family members or friends may do the Scripture readings, bring up the gifts which may include some personal item of the deceased (such as a hammer, a photograph—whatever characterizes the deceased in the eyes of the family), read the Prayers of the Faithful, and give a eulogy at the end of Mass. Parish community members may do the wake service and provide hospitality at the wake or after the funeral. Dying, like living, is a community affair.

How Strict?

Meanwhile, you hear horror stories of priests refusing to baptize the babies of non-practicing or non-married parents, or of a pastor who won't let some kid be confirmed because he didn't attend all the classes, or of those who would not bury someone because they didn't use collection envelopes. It seems there are many hoops people have to jump through to get something done in the church.

On the one hand, you have the priest who wants to protect the sacraments from being merely a a cultural custom, like giving a bottle of scotch for Christmas. "Of course," these parents think, "we'll have our baby baptized Catholic even if we haven't been to church since *we* were." Then you have the non-practicing or non-conforming parent or individual who has his or her own agenda and can't understand what the fuss is all about. All that I can say here is that it is a dilemma. That is, as one book's title puts it, how do we challenge people without crushing them? Things have changed. People *do* have responsibilities. The parish exists to supplement people, not to substitute for them. People shouldn't just "use" the parish for ceremonial occasions. That's hurtful and demeaning, like the parish coming to you only when it wants money.

On the other hand, people have a journey and they have a story. They should be heard. The lesson seems to be that we need better mechanisms to help us to listen and to be gentle. We need to learn how to challenge without turning away, to invite without rejection. It's an art, and if you have ever been on the receiving end of a clerical negative I suggest that, in calmer moments, you make an appointment to talk things over. Maybe every parish or region needs a grievance board made up of clergy and laity who will review conflicts in the area of parish policy and rules. There is something to be said on both sides. People skilled in conflict management could do a lot here in finding a middle ground between reasonable rules and personal stories. Rules always need to be flexible in honoring people's circumstances and special needs. Still, people should be aware of how necessary it is to be more than skin-deep Catholics in these urgent times. To sum it up: As far as the rules go, leniency should be the norm, fidelity the challenge, dialogue the procedure.

Resources

A New Look at the Sacraments by William J. Bausch (Twenty-Third Publications, 1983). Will bring you up to date on the latest "look."

The Marginal Catholic: Challenge, Don't Crush by Joseph Champlin (Ave Maria Press, 1989). Might be a good gift to give to your tormentor.

A Catholic Bill of Rights edited by Leonard Swidler and Herbert O'Brien (Sheed & Ward, 1988). Brief essays on what official Canon Law of the church says about your rights.

Chapter 6

ALL THOSE PEOPLE!

Circle vs Pyramid

A current—very current—joke tells the story of a wizened old priest shuffling to the pulpit to announce to his people, "The bishop has extended the retirement age to 103, so I'll be with you till October." The joke reflects what everyone knows, what you perhaps have sensed in your parish: There is a priest shortage. You may remember a rectory full of priests, but those full rectories exist no more. Actually, the dwindling has been going on quite some time, long before Vatican II, but since Vatican II the shortage has accelerated to crisis proportions.

Whatever the reasons, you may observe that we now have a number of lay people doing jobs that once were thought to be the exclusive task of the clergy. On thinking about this, your first instinct might be, "Well, once the shortage is over, then the priests can retrieve their old jobs and the people can go back to 'praying, obeying, and paying.' Right?" Wrong. That is to underestimate the genuine and lasting recovery of an ancient truism: Being church is a communal enterprise.

A second look at Scripture and tradition turns up a lot of "lay" participation. The gospels speak of Zacchaeus, Simon's mother-in-law, Jairus, Martha, Mary, Lazarus, the woman at the well. They all stayed put in their villages and towns to spread the Good News of the gospel. In St. Paul's epistles we come across those strange Greek and Latin names all over the area: Priscilla and Aquila, Straphina and Trophosa, Andronicus and Julia—all husband and wife teams. Then there are Nerius and his sister, Hemes and his brother, Rufus and his mother, Urban, Cornelius, Narcissus, Stephanus, Phoebe, and a host of others. These are not household names, but they give testimony to the reality of the shared ministry of all the people. St. Paul was even quite explicit. In 1 Corinthians (12:4–6, 27–30) he wrote: "You are the Body of Christ and individually members of it. And God appointed in the church first apostles, second prophets, third teachers, then workers of miracles, then healers, helpers, administrators, speakers in various kinds of tongues."

It was a busy church in the early centuries; everyone was involved—until slowly but surely collaboration began to unravel and the circle (to use a helpful image) got hammered into a pyramid. So much so, that were I to ask you to diagram power and authority in the church, you would come up with the diagram on page 57.

Likely your concept of the parish would be a subsidiary of the Vatican much like your local Chevrolet dealership is the subsidiary of General Motors main headquarters. All pyramid thinking.

Loss and Recovery

It's a long story we can't tell here, except to say that through a lot of coincidental pressures of history, the Christian mission that started off and remained a common enterprise of all baptized people (circle) began to become more and more centralized into the hands of the clergy (pyramid). The cler-

```
                    God
                   Jesus
               Peter the pope
                 Apostles
                 Cardinals
                  Bishops
                Monsignors
                  Priests
                  Deacons
       Religious Brothers and Sisters
                   Laity
                  Women
```

gy, to be sure, were needed and essential, but with them slowly absorbing *all* roles and gifts and tasks to themselves throughout the centuries, they produced in the end an active-passive imbalance: The clergy and religious were the active members of the church and the laity were the passive. You get a kind of highpoint of this attitude in the words of Pope Pius X at the beginning of this century. In one of his encyclicals he wrote, "The church is essentially an unequal society. That is, it is a society formed by pastors and flock.... As far as the multitude is concerned, they have no other duty than to let themselves be led." How does that grate on your democratic, American sensibilities? As students, we had our own subversive version:

The pope is the servant of the servants of God. A bishop is the servant of the servant of the servants of God. A priest is the servant of the servant of the servant of the servants of God. A deacon is the servant of the servant of the servant of the servant of the servants of God. A layman is a rich man with a servant problem.

Vatican II, looking back at history, was determined to set things straight. First, it laid down the principle that was a "universal call to holiness." Sanctity was not the preserve of the priest, sister, and monk. You'd get that impression if you look at the official list of canonized saints. Can you name more than three saints who were *not* popes, priests, religious, or monks? The truth is, holiness is democratic, meant for all and available for all in their everyday lives.

Second, along with this thought, Vatican II reminded us that the main sacrament is baptism. That's where we are all incorporated into the church and all receive the mission to evangelize, to live, share, and preach the gospel. Priestly ordination ordains one to leadership, but a leadership that is targeted at helping all *their* commitments, to use *their* gifts. All the people are the church.

To make sure everyone understood, Vatican II taught—loud and clear—things like this:

> The lay apostolate is a participation in the saving mission of the church itself. Through baptism and confirmation, all are commissioned to that apostolate by the Lord himself. . . . [People] carry out *their own part* in the mission of the whole Christian people with respect to the church and the world. . . . Pastors also know that they themselves were not meant by Christ to shoulder alone the entire saving mission of the church towards the world. On the contrary, they understand that it is their noble duty so to shepherd the faithful and recognize their services and charismatic gifts, that *all* according to their proper role may cooperate in this common undertaking with one heart. . . . The laity share the universal call to holiness with those in religious life. . . . they permeate society with the leaven of the gospel. They are the salt of the earth drawing the world to Christ. (italics added)

Ministry

Those ringing words ushered in the changes you are observing, perhaps with puzzlement and amazement. If empowerment is the corporate buzz word, ministry is the church's. It's a code word that sums up the sense of everyone's mission, not by delegation, but by right. It is often used uncritically, but that just shows how new our recovery is. Anyway, all sorts of lay people are "in ministry"—and this, not by virtue of the priest shortage, but by virtue of just being Christian (baptized). And that accounts for "all those people" in our chapter title. All those people being active, doing things, proclaiming the Scripture, distributing communion, leading song, greeting the faithful, heading up church committees and parish councils, visiting hospitals and nursing homes, teaching religion, sometimes preaching, leading prayer groups, reaching out. That's their right. They too are the church. And if you have been away a long time, it can be a revelation to see how active your friends and neighbors are.

One man, a journalist, had been away from the church a long, long time. He dropped out at 17 because at 15 a priest preached distressfully against altar boys and refused to give communion to some (including himself); at 16 a priest punished some schoolboy infringement by requiring some boys (including himself) to lie spread-eagle in the school entrance hall where he then walked across their fingers. Talk about dysfunction! So he dropped out. Anyway, years later his mother came to visit him and asked to be taken to church. He had no idea where a church was, but he finally found a parish (of which he is now a member) and was amazed. He wrote:

It was a breathtaking experience, for here was a community in which Christianity seemed vividly alive. Its liturgy was couched in accents of everyday language.

The activities in the church hall afterwards were as vibrant as those in the Mass room. It was driven by lay women and men, served by a parish priest determined not to rule but to enable others and bring out their fullest talents. It reached outside the church building with all manner of service and ministry. It celebrated the glory of life and worked with unflagging commitment against injustice in the world. This was not the church I had left.

Paul Vallely (*The Tablet*, March 13, 1993)

It would be wonderful to hope that you have had the same experience, but even if you haven't, the principle is there. History and theology have reasserted themselves and once more we are aware that we are all in this together. We are, in the retrieved phrase of Vatican II, a "People of God." All of us.

Authority

But being in all this together, being a "People of God" has shifted the role of authority too. Your parents may remember a very different concept of church authority than what you are experiencing. That's because they were on the receiving end of a lot of turbulent history. You might recall that in Chapter 2 we saw many upheavals buffeting the church. In the late 1700s and all throughout the 1800s the church was under siege. Napoleon, Garibaldi, Bismarck, and others took from the Vatican whatever political power it had left. Then the new philosophies suggested new ways of viewing life and that undermined the church's moral authority. So the church became very defensive. It centralized in Rome as never before and cemented its position of vertical authority in 1870 when the First Vatican Council declared the doctrine of papal infallibility.

As we said before, national and local churches began to

be viewed as outlets for the major headquarters in Rome. Authority was distinctly vertical from the pope on down. Everything got stamped with church authority from the serious (It's a mortal sin to miss Mass on Sunday) to the trivial (It's a mortal sin to eat a hotdog on Friday) because all were leveled by the one measurement: contempt for church authority.

The Europeans, being closer to the source of power, were more nonchalant and tended to take things with a grain of salt. But not the Americans. The Vatican was concerned that this new nation of immigrants would take democratic ideals too seriously and so it was felt necessary to instill in them a great sense of loyalty and obedience. You may not know that the first two Catholic bishops in the United States were elected democratically by the clergy. Rome soon put a stop to that. American Catholics must submit to authority as mediated through the church centralized at Rome. And that was that. This attitude was not entirely successful, because we witnessed early conflicts between clergy and laity and a schism here and there over the question of authority. Still, obedience rather than rebellion became the American Catholic standard. And it had its points. No dissent was permitted—black was black, white was white. You knew where you stood. And if you didn't have the answers, the local pastor did.

But all that changed in your lifetime and even in the lifetime of your parents. First, a peek into Scripture and history again brought different perspectives on authority in the church. Jesus himself clearly taught that however authority was to be exercised in his church, it would be quite different from the world. In Luke's gospel (22:25–26) he says, "Among pagans it is the kings who rule over them. . . . This is not to happen to you. Rather, let the greatest among you be as the least, as the one who serves." At the Last Supper, after washing his disciples' feet, Jesus said, "Do you under-

stand what I have done to you? You call me 'Master' and
'Lord' and rightly; for so I am. But if I, Master and Lord,
have washed your feet, you should wash each other's feet. I
have given you an example so that you may do what I have
done to you" (John 13:12–15). In another place he says, "The
Son of Man has not come to be served, but to serve." So
Jesus refused to describe his own mission and his own authority in terms of ruling over others.

Evolution

The first church followed his advice. When Judas's place
had to be filled, the disciples voted on a replacement. St.
Paul felt free to differ with St. Peter. The official leaders
were sensitive to the needs, opinions, and advice of others,
for they knew the Spirit would blow where it will. But, of
course, things got more complicated as the church ex-
panded to Europe and finally was legitimized by a Roman
emperor. Then it took on the trappings and structures of civil authorities with the pope being equivalent to the emperor,
the bishops equivalent to the governors, and the priests
equivalent to mayors.

Still, for most centuries, with no strong central control
(Rome), sections of the church were quite autonomous. This
is seen, for example, in the fact that the bishops were elected
by the clergy or the emperor or the people (Bishop St.
Ambrose was publicly acclaimed bishop by the mob). A
2nd-century Christian document says, "Let him be ordained
as bishop who has been chosen by all the people." A 5th-
century pope, Celestine, wrote, "Let a bishop not be im-
posed upon the people whom they do not want." It really
wasn't until 1917 that the pope took over entirely the appointment of bishops. This means that by that time in history he had become a papal CEO. Authority in the church
was from top to bottom, with no discussion or consultation.

But along came Vatican II with its years and years of research and homework behind it. Relying heavily on Scripture and history, it said in effect, let's return authority and power of the local churches and let's admit that, in fact, "The Holy Spirit is present in the faithful of every rank." So, while not denying the unique position of the pope, Vatican II presented a more collegial way of ruling. The fallout from this is a synod of bishops whom the pope consults, priests' senates whom the bishop consults, pastoral councils of lay people whom the bishop also consults, and parish councils whom the pastor consults.

Cynicism

All this has come none too soon; attitudes toward authority were rapidly and radically changing in our country for better and for worse because society itself was in turmoil. "Don't trust anyone over 30" was Woodstock's cry. Abuses of civil authority horrified the public as police clubbed civil rights activists. Presidents Nixon, Johnson, and Kennedy consistently lied to the people. From Watergate to Irangate people became suspicious of all politicians and all authority. On the church front, the birth control ruling in 1968 shook many Catholics' faith in church authority as they openly disagreed with the conclusion that birth control is morally wrong. (Latest polls show 87 percent disagree with the church's official stand.) The Vatican's public curbing of well-known theologians rubbed the American sense of the right to dissent the wrong way.

For Catholic North Americans who take for granted the dynamics of consultation, consensus, and negotiation, the Vatican comes off as heavy-handed when it issues unilateral pronouncements. And recent revelations of pedophilia among priests with diocesan cover-ups have further shaken confidence in church authority (saying one thing, doing another). For Baby Boomers, raised in a culture that is highly individualistic, enshrines individual freedom and autonomy, and has elevated personal choice to the highest moral stature, authority is a big issue and a bigger one for those returning to an "authority" church. Still, for all the self-directed language of choice and autonomy, the problem is that there is a need to answer this question: To whom or to what can I turn for reliable answers to religious questions?

The church; that's the response. Most people *want* church authority, *but* an authority that is credible, one that takes their insights and experience into account. After all, people like yourself recognize that there is a dark side to authority (being like Stalin). Remember, it is the radical left that has used authority in its worst form: from the communists to the Black Panthers to the Politically Correct watchdogs; they have killed or removed those who would not submit to their authority. The reactionary right prefers the language of personal rights and liberties.

But there is also a dark side to individualism (doing your own thing at the expense of others). Catholics (like yourself, I suspect) who are sincerely concerned with religion in their lives expect the church to guide and enlighten them. For the simple fact is that as well as being called to be free, we understand that we are also called to be answerable to each other, to be in solidarity. It makes sense that we should have a community to hold us accountable and to recognize that through baptism we are indeed but one member of a universal body and therefore just can't make up things to suit ourselves.

So even if we don't relate well to the church as an institution or its rules, we try to respect the church's ideals. It's just that most returnees (and all Catholics for that matter) want the church to be a little more human and show a little more leeway in trying to come to terms with them. In fact, a recent Gallup poll shows an interesting contradiction that underscores this attitude. Eighty-seven percent of Catholics think the church should permit couples to make their own decision about forms of birth control, and at the same time 84 percent think Pope John Paul II—who never fails to condemn birth control—is doing a good job leading the church!

In any case, there are many signs of change in this whole area of ministry and authority. We already mentioned the bishops' synod and priests' senates. And the people with authority are changing. In fact, what is happening in the church is what is happening in corporate life. We're experiencing a new kind of leadership. It's not that leadership itself is passe or invalid. On the contrary. It is more critical than ever. It's the *style* of leadership that has changed. CEOs, as the Japanese have shown us, must *empower* (the buzz word) the employees. Employees must have creative input into the product.

You have gurus writing all kinds of best sellers on leadership: Tom Peter's *Liberation Management*, Peter Drucker's *Managing for the 90s and Beyond*, Fred Fidler's *Situational Leadership*, to name a few. They all give the same message: Leadership respects the person, enables the employee, notes differences, provides for creativity, applies the principles of subsidiarity, and so on. The church is on the same track although, like corporate life itself, the application is uneven and perhaps even regressive. Nevertheless, it's there. So if you want to make a difference, run for your parish council! You can dissent and remain a faithful Catholic—but be sure you do your homework.

So, who are all those people who suddenly have appeared while you were gone? They're your friends and neighbors. They are you. Welcome aboard to being church!

Resources

Ministry in the Church: A Historical and Pastoral Approach by Paul Bernier (Twenty-Third Publications, 1992).

Laity's Mission in the Local Church by Leonard Doohan (Harper & Row, 1986). Like it says.

Collaborative Ministry: Communion, Contention, Commitment by Norman P. Cooper ((Paulist Press, 1993). A good understanding of ministry and a good plan for its implementation.

New Parish Ministries: Laity and Religious on Parish Staffs by Philip Murnion, et al. (National Pastoral Life Center, 1992). A survey detailing the many, many ministries in the church. Informative.

Chapter 7

THE PARISH

Centrality

For most people like yourself, the parish is what you identify as "the church." Most don't care what the Vatican does,
or the pope or the bishop. They're important, make good
copy, but they're remote. No, the average Catholic's and
non-Catholic's experience of what they think the church is
really about is relayed through the local parish. Here the
pastor is more significant than the pope, the sister more
than the bishop, and the secretary more than the monsignor.
I once wrote that the parish

> is the first ecclesiastical hand that rocks the organized
> religious cradle. . . . the simple arithmetic is that before
> any human being gets to meet his or her chaplain, cam-
> pus minister, retreat master or tribunal official, that in-
> dividual first has to pass through the influence of the
> local parish community.

That's still true.

For the most part, I must say, the people love their parishes. And if they don't—well, these days, they are permitted by law to parish hop till they find one they like. The
best way to find a good parish is not to ask the pastor or
read their mission statement, but to ask the everyday people
who go there, and to attend a few times to catch the spirit of
the community.

Styles
Of course, parishes, like individuals, differ in style, emphasis, and mission. Here are some styles you'll discover
around the country—a quick, thumb-nail guide to tell you
what to look for.

1. *The traditionalistic parish.* Here people are consumers.
They come to get what they need from a parish run by an
autocratic pastor. He may indeed be a nice man, but all
power and all decisions rest with him. He is the end-spout
of what has been poured down from the pope to the bishop
to him. And he obediently pours it out to you. And what he
passes down is the old tradition as he understands it. He
gives the people a feeling of being in touch with "the good
old days" before everything went haywire. And that's a gift
many people appreciate. There's not much shared, collaborative ministry, though.

2. *The charismatic parish.* Here I mean, really, the pastor
who is charismatic. He is a gifted and exciting leader, open
to new ideas, while holding to the best of the old. The parish
is alive with his gifts. The trouble is, of course, that when he
moves, the whole enterprise collapses. Be wary.

3. *The collaborative parish.* This style of parish engages the
talents and gifts of all the parishioners. You'll sense own-
ership, activity, prayerfulness. Look into this one.

4. *The CFS parish.* Those initials stand for the Chronic Fa-
tigue Syndrome. Here it's parish life on the edge: overactive,

frantic, many activities, but no "center." Everyone's exhausted from running and doing all day long. An exciting place, but it will wear you down. Avoid.

5. *The Sherwin Williams* parish. A little of this and a little of that, but not much of anything. There's not much enabling, no sense of mission. One thin coat covers all. Enough said.

6. *The factional family parish.* Polarization is the key here. The pastor is Vatican I, the associate is Vatican II, and there is civil war that spills over to the parish at large with hoards of people on either side writing to the bishop to denounce the other side. There's much energy, all right, but it's all destructive. Keep away from this one.

7. *The "nothin'-honey" parish.* "What's going on at the parish this week?" You've got it: "Nothin', honey." Sacraments are offered but with bare bones efforts and ceremony. Dysfunctional staff. That sort of thing. You can do better.

Community

You will often see nowadays a parish advertising itself as "St. Benedict's Community." The inclusion of the last word instead of "parish" is an attempt to remind folk that the parish is not just another club. It's a way of life, a way people interact among themselves and reach out to others. It's also an attempt to serve warning that members should be contributors, not just consumers. That is to say, as we mentioned in Chapter 6, that involvement is important. The parish community is a living enterprise and requires many talents and many hands. It suggests that you should not only support your parish financially (alas, Catholics are the richest single religious group in America next to the Jews and among the lowest contributors; they have no sense of stewardship and tithing), but morally and physically. You have talents to help "build up the Body of Christ," as St. Paul puts it.

Volunteerism

We're talking about volunteerism, of course. You might recall that the most enduring slogan of George Bush's campaign in 1988 was his call for "a thousand points of light." He urged all Americans to get involved, to personally participate in the needs of others. Bill Clinton picked up that cause and phrase as well. After all, it is well to remember that it was the spirit of volunteerism in 19th-century America that is credited with providing support and agitation to end slavery, educate women, popularize temperance, and generally prick the nation's conscience on a range of social issues.

We look back with nostalgia on that era as we look at our own work schedules that seem to fill every nook and cranny of our lives. Volunteerism seems such a luxury and the prospect of squandering our precious free time at the parish or with people trapped in dire circumstances is daunting, not to mention depressing. We don't want to add more stress to our stressful lives.

But does this have to be? There's an interesting book called *The Healing Power of Doing Good* by Allan Luks (Fawcett Columbine, 1991). He found out that instead of finding themselves dragged down by others' problems and challenges, volunteers felt "pumped up," exuberant, happier, healthier, and more stress-free. In short, he found the equivalent to the "runner's high": the "helper's high." And this high endured over the years and went across the range of age and sex. He also found scientific documentation that volunteering reduced blood pressure, stomach acid levels, and even cholesterol counts—and even brought about the response known as the "Mother Teresa Effect," that is, even watching someone else's actively doing good for others increased immunoglobin, the body's first line of defense against the cold virus.

Perhaps you saw the movie "Sister Act." If not, rent it. It's hilarious. You might recall that a casino singer (Whoopi

Goldberg) witnesses a gangster's execution and agrees to testify. The police hustle her off to an inner-city convent in San Francisco and have her pose as a nun to keep her safe in hiding before the trial. In no time, sparks fly between this rather unconventional casino-singing "nun" and the real sisters in their protected fortress of a convent. Yet when she starts helping out the convent's inept choir, the hermetically sealed church and its surrounding neighborhood are transformed. The convent's sanctuary, once closed off to the dilapidated world around it, suddenly becomes a "happening" in the neighborhood. The doors are unbarred and the windows flung open as both church and neighborhood are renewed.

If you want the traditional translation of this movie, go no further than the Prayer of St. Francis:

O Master, grant that I may never seek
So much to be consoled as to console;
To be understood as to understand,
To be loved as to love with all my soul.
For it is in pardoning that we are pardoned,
In giving to all that we receive
And in dying that we are born to eternal life.

The Pitch

You may see all this as a long wind-up to get you involved in your parish, and that's partly true. But I would remind you of the following facts:

1. The parish will only be as good as you make it good. You can't leave it all up to the pastor. The church needs you.

2. In spite of your business, you have talents to offer and gifts to share, even if they are short, one-shot events. You can join the finance committee, the parish council, or be Eucharistic minister, lector, or usher. You can run a dance,

help with the youth, or plant some flowers. You and your family can fill food baskets that the parish collects at Thanksgiving and Christmas and deliver them to needy families. These are very limited in commitment. Or you can go for the longer run: Teach religion to children, teach an adult course, or be a consultant in your field of expertise. You've got a "Sister Act" somewhere.

3. Remember, through baptism you are the church. You are co-responsible for it and for others. You can't be a good Catholic without being concerned about the poor and oppressed.

4. Parent or not, married or not, your involvement builds up precious memories for the generation after you. You should not underestimate this. All surveys (in addition to common sense) show that involved adults are wonderful role models for children. They sense religion in action and adopt the values implicit in it. Or, to use a practical example, if teens seem insensitive to the plight of the poor, the solution is not to harangue them. The solution is to arrange for them to work in a soup kitchen—and see adults there too.

5. You might want to go further. There are superior lay volunteer programs for families, singles, and young adults that provide opportunities to go to the depressed areas of this country and other countries to give some (supervised) time to the poor and needy. Again, if kids are into the designer clothes and the Absolute Reebok syndrome, you might have them work at the K-Mart for a year or send them with a group to Appalachia.

Tensions in the Assembly

If you're a returning Catholic from the Baby Boomer era, it's only fair to say that you may experience some conflict in the parish, certainly not open physical conflict, but rather a conflict in style, expectation, and reception. After all, you have to remember that you have a wide range of people in the average parish: people who have been there before you, perhaps some who pioneered the parish, built it, and have a vested interest in it.

Also, you have people whose age and concerns are vastly divergent. There are those under 30 whose lives have been shaped by television, broken homes, and two-wage-earner families who know nothing but change. You have the 30-to-40 crowd that remembers Vietnam and Woodstock and affluence and who, though low in commitment, are high in compassion. You have the 40-to-50 group who are being crunched by a recessive economy and are driven by career success and security. Then you have those 50-and-over folk who have lived through one or two World Wars and an economic depression and worry about financial stability and diminishing vigor. Add to this mix those fellow parishioners harboring deep liberal or conservative sentiments, and you can see the possibilities for tension in the assembly. You can also see, I hope, the incredible task of any pastor who must shepherd all this diversity.

Besides returning to a quite diverse parish with vying interests (which you have to learn to respect), you might run into some unspoken and unconscious resistance. For example, the people of the parish are glad to have you, but not in the power structure of the parish. You can do all kinds of jobs and volunteer for wonderful ministries, but the Old Guard might keep you out of decision positions, such as a place on the parish council or finance committee. Your suggestions for new programs (for example, child care) might fall on deaf ears because it's too novel and "we've always done it this way"; and, besides, that's not their agenda.

The Old Guard is often apt to emphasize rules, while you might emphasize relationships, and so you can't quite understand each other. They may be dismayed at your self-centeredness and look askance at your male-female equality roles, while you wonder where they're coming from. They may want the parish to remain as it always was: back in the 19th century, while you want to bring it into the 20th. They may not want you and your family to use the parish hall and mess it all up. And you alarm them: If too many of you return, they "don't know anybody any more." And they resent it if you innocently sit in *their* pew on Sunday.

All this means that you may have to be (charitably) persistent in getting parish programs that suit you and your family's needs, in making your schedule known, that is, that you can't come out every night for a meeting like your parents did and that therefore the parish ought to have short-term, quality events you can attend. Feel free to suggest that the music at Mass is all right, but there are some contemporary pieces that are very good, too. And remember that your parish family is like your own family: There are diverse personalities and interests, but a common bond of love that makes it work. In time, they'll welcome "new blood," and most pastors will accept all the creative suggestions and talents they can get.

Conclusion

I've tried to give you, a returning Catholic, a sense that the parish, too, has changed. It's no longer a "service station" rationing out grace at baptism, wedding, and funeral times (but you'll still find a few around like that). The parish is not the quiet, passive place some of your parents experienced, though far from all. It's not there for ceremonial occasions. The parish is, as we have said before, a communal enterprise. It's the locale where most of us find support and nourishment for the Christian life, and that requires not only good leadership but members who are involved and want to deepen their faith and pass it on to the next generation. It's a living community, the place of encouragement as well as diversity, the place where we break open the Word of God and know Jesus in the breaking of the bread.

Resources

The Catholic Way of Life by David Byers, Neil Parent, and B. Allison Smith (Paulist National Evangelization Association, 1990). A fine handbook. If you don't get any other book, get this one.

Dealing With Diversity: A Guide for Parish Leaders by Greg Dues (Twenty-Third Publications, 1989). Practical for recognizing the causes of and solutions for such problems.

The Hands-On Parish: Reflections and Suggestions for Fostering Community by William J. Bausch (Twenty-Third Publications, 1989). A hundred ideas to make your parish live.

The *Lay Volunteers Mission Opportunities Directory* is an annual resource handbook put out by the International Liaison of Lay Volunteers in Mission, 4121 Harewood Road, N.E., Washington, D.C. 20017. It's a network of placements for volunteers here and abroad. From the table of contents: Foreign Placement, Married Couples, Married/ Single Parents with Dependents, Over 55 Years of Age, 18 years of Age, Non-Live-in Community Housing, Short-Term Programs (three weeks or less), etc. Take a look.

Who Will Miss Me If I Don't Go to Church? by Susan Heyboer O'Keefe (Paulist Press). For children, but helpful to their parents as well.

Chapter 8

SHARING THE WORD

Scripture

One of the characteristics of the post-Vatican II church has been the retrieval of Scripture. Not that the church has never used Scripture; after all, the church wrote (at least the New Testament part) and gave us the Scripture and collected and approved the books that went into the little library we call the Bible. It's just that when the Protestant Reformation came along disparaging the sacraments, ritual, and the church and extolling the Scripture as the only rule of faith, then the church reacted by playing down Scripture and extolling the sacraments, ritual, and the church. It was a matter of emphasis. So the Protestants went to church toting their Bibles and the Catholics went to church toting their missals. The Protestants knew chapter and verse of the Good Book. The Catholics knew the seven sacraments, the six commandments of the church, and what three things make a sin mortal. The net result was that the Bible became a symbol of division.

But all that has changed. There has been tremendous research and discoveries concerning Scripture, and the church has been in the forefront of that biblical research. Besides this, on November 18, 1965, the Second Vatican Council officially issued a position paper on the Bible urging its study, reading, and preaching. The result has been that the church has reworked its rituals and sacraments to include heavy doses of Scripture. Even at Mass you have three readings of the Bible so that in every three-year cycle the entire Bible will have been proclaimed. So the combination of ceasing to react to the Protestants (and indeed, in true ecumenism, to work with them in the areas of the Bible) and new insights and discoveries have once more made the Catholic church a biblical church. And that's why you'll discover Scripture in every area of church life. And that includes much Scripture in the books your children study in Catholic schools or in their parish religion classes.

Word Groups

But the revival of Scripture, along with certain other events on the world scene, have produced another phenomenon: the Small Base Community, or Small Christian Communities. Call them what you will, these are small groups of Christians, anywhere from 9 or 10 to 25 or 30, who meet regularly to read Scripture and discuss its relevance to our times. This movement began in Latin America and Africa among the poor. The shortage of priests, oppression, and poverty led these people to seek more deeply how they could change an unjust society from principles grounded in sacred Scripture. These groups are lay led; men and women bring their experiences to the word of God. And suddenly the world is learning how the peasants in a Brazilian barrio understand the story of the Lazarus at the door of the rich; how a feminist reads the story of the woman at the well; how blacks read the parable of the Good Samaritan. And we all begin to realize what demands discipleship makes on us and how intimate is the relationship between faith and doing justice.

In North America there have been the beginnings of such groups. They are very popular in the southwest among the Hispanics, but they have moved everywhere. Some of you may have heard of the *Renew* process, which is basically a shared study of the Scripture. But there are many others. Your parish or a nearby one may have similar groups. They are well worth your time. The simple conviction among all believers is that Sunday is not enough. Not nearly enough. To gather another time in groups of 9 or 10 to break open God's word is called for. This, of course, is not done haphazardly. There are excellent books and programs and fine facilitator training sessions. And, as we indicated before, this is lay "ministry," a lay-led activity. Your parents had the sodalities and Rosary Altar societies, the Christian Family Movement and Cursillo. These groups are alive and potent, but I suspect that the small Christian Community might have more of an appeal to you.

Here are some sharings from these groups:

+ I lost my job. After 30 years! The roof caved in. It was the worst thing that ever happened. My family, my faith got me through it.
+ So, if there's a labor meeting, I show up. It's my vocation to be there.
+ A group of us began to get together on Saturday mornings to talk about where God has been in our lives that week. These were high-powered people. They began to open up, to trust one another. I got help on concrete problems. It was the best church I ever had.
+ There used to be two choices for Catholic women: Get married or become a nun. There has to be another way. I'm a successful business woman, single and on my own.

The Lord put me in touch with other loving people who need me and who let me need them.

So this is what is on the Catholic scene now. Another startling and Spirit-filled growth that happened while you were gone. But, as you should suspect by now, these small groups are not something new. Remember, we saw that for the first four hundred years Christians met in homes ("house-churches") to pray Scripture and break bread. For example, St. Paul addresses an epistle written around 56 A.D. to Philemon, his fellow workers, and "the church at your house." In a letter to the Galatians, St. Paul writes to the house-based *churches* of Galatia. St. Peter's letters were circulated among the house-churches.

In fact, if you want a little bit of Catholic trivia, the Greek word for house-church is *oikos*. When you got a number of house-churches together, you eventually formed a *par oikos* ("above the house-church") and when you got a number of *par oikos* together you got a *dia oikos*, or "across the house church." You don't have to be a Greek scholar to see the words "parish" and "diocese" here. The point is that the main building block of the church made up of parishes and dioceses is the house-church unit. And that's what basically these small sharing groups are. We are simply returning to our New Testament roots when we meet in small groups to read and share the word of God.

In fact, now that immigrant Catholicism with all of its necessary paternalism and nurturing is dead, and cohesive Catholicism with its isolation and emphasis on authority is gone, we are into a kind of modern evangelical Catholicism where we center on Jesus and Scripture to the point that we no longer ask exclusively, "What does the church teach?" as "What would Jesus do?" Anyway, see if your parish or one nearby has such Scripture groups. If not, start your own. They will prove powerful for you and your family.

Marketplace Spirituality

These remarks logically lead us to note another significant change in the church. We hinted at it before and now briefly we want to underscore it a bit more. We said that one of the calls to more lay involvement in being church was the reminder of the Vatican Council of our "universal call to holiness." The emphasis was on universal. *All* were called, not just the clergy and religious. And here I want to correct an impression I may have given in Chapter 6; that is, the call is to ministry and that ministry has to do with being busy in church affairs. That, indeed, is one arena of faith in action. But it's not the place for most of us. The everyday world is our arena of sanctity, where we grow in true holiness and work out our salvation. Our families and places of schooling and employment constitute the main context of where we live and die as Christians. Here it is that we are to be holy and to witness to the presence of Christ in the world.

One businessman has the sense of it when he writes:

This is our vocation, the vocation of the Catholic Christian layman and laywoman. . . . It is a high calling. We are the church in the world. We are the key social agents of church in the world. We are the religious insiders, inside secular society and its institutions. Without our knowledge, skill, power and commitment the church cannot fulfill its mission, cannot be herself. Without us, without an awakened laity, the church is in danger of becoming a weak and ineffective voice, confined to the sidelines and backwaters of American life.

John McDermott (*The New American Catholic*, 1986)

Another layman wrote:

We frequently tend to compartmentalize our lives! Perhaps we must listen to the dismissal charge [at the end of Mass] and focus less on the "ended" and more on the exhortation to "love and serve the Lord." As Catholic Christians in the work world we must carry the gospel message into our workplace and communities.

The revolution for you as a returning Catholic is to sense that you have a vocation, a calling. Formerly that word vocation was confined to the call to be a priest or sister or brother. But the fact is that through baptism we are all called to be disciples. You are the church in the world. It's as simple and profound as that. It's no longer the clergy-lay world of your parents in the sense that there were passive (laity) and active (clergy) apostles. You can no longer leave salvation and evangelization up to "Father" or "Sister." Rather, you are collaborators in living out and sharing the Good News. This means that all of us must take the risk of acting differently, to be labeled as serious believers. Butcher, baker, or candlestick maker, you must bring the principles of fairness, justice, and charity to your task. Where you are, the church is.

And you thought that returning to the church was like renewing your membership in the Kiwanis: Pay your dues, attend some meetings, and reap some benefits! Now you've discovered you did not return to an organization separate from you. You have returned to being the organization itself, being the Body of Christ, being church.

While you were gone, much has changed. More accurately put, while you were gone much has been recovered: Scripture, sharing, and discipleship.

Resources

Dangerous Memories: House Churches and Our American Story by Bernard J. Lee and Michael A. Cowan (Sheed & Ward, 1986). A brief book that does a fine job on examining small groups.

Good Things Happen: Experiencing Community in Small Groups by Dick Westley (Twenty-Third Publications, 1992).

Radical Christian Communities by Thomas Rausch, S.J. (Liturgical Press, 1990).

Buena Vista (P.O. Box 5474, Arvae CO 80005) is a national network of people devoted to the formation of small communities.

Laity Stirring the Church by Dolores R. Lecky (Fortress Press, 1987).

Practical Spirituality for Lay People by Dolores R. Lecky (Sheed & Ward, 1987).

Confident & Competent: A Challenge for the Lay Church by William L. Droel and Gregory Augustine Pierce (Ave Maria Press, 1987). Being church in the world.

Scripture Today by John Boyle, S.J. (Thomas More Press, 1990).

Reading the New Testament by Pheme Perkins (Paulist Press, 2nd ed., 1988). A general good text for college level.

There is a fine study series of the Bible from Little Rock for adults, teens, and children. Ask your pastor about it.

PART THREE

THE CHALLENGE

Chapter 9

UNFINISHED BUSINESS

In this next to last chapter, our aims are modest. We want to explore with returning Catholics like yourself four aspects of what we might call "unfinished business." More precisely we simply want to identify them and comment on them. Actually, this should not surprise us that there might be unfinished business. After all, life is unfinished. Which means it's an ongoing journey. So, too, the church. It is, we are, in the words of Vatican II, a Pilgrim People. This implies that we have to rely on the Spirit to guide us as new and challenging developments confront us as we journey onward.

It would be naive to think that you have returned to a completed or perfect church. If you ever find one, as Andrew Greeley has observed, by all means join it. Of course, the moment you do, it won't be perfect any more. All this is a way of saying that we have to live in a certain tension as new forms break through and the gospel is translated anew for new times. Meanwhile, we try not to polarize as we attempt to dialogue in charity with those we disagree with.

You have returned. So have others. Still others have never left. Each has his or her own ideas of what it means to be church and where we ought to be going. You have to expect that; you have to expect unfinished business.

Singles

You may balk, as I do (being single), to find being single listed under unfinished business. But the statistical fact is that the large number of singles is a new sociological fact and we don't know how to deal with it. In former times, most people got married and stayed married. Today, being single is the fastest growing category that shows up on the population spread sheet. For instance, in 1983 the average age for marrying in the United States was 18 to 23. In 1991, the average age was 27. This is due to more options today: financial ability to stay single, divorce, a two-income family that demands longer singleness to save, the growing live-in relationships, single parents, sperm-donor babies, group housing, etc. Fewer than 27 percent of the households today consist of father, mother, and children. Four out of ten babies today are born with no father living in the household. Whatever the reason, some estimate that by the year 2000, the majority of adults—52 percent—in the United States will be single. Perhaps you are among them.

For us in the organizational end, the agenda is how to handle singles in a church traditionally geared for traditional families. For singles who are in a kind of social limbo and who have returned to the church, the agenda is precisely that of unfinished business, that is, how to get the church—and society for that matter—to recognize them and to assimilate them. And here the local parish can be critical. You will have to challenge your parish to consider you in the mainstream of parish life. You should freely be in any and all of the liturgical ministries (Eucharistic ministers, lectors, etc.), organizational structures (parish council), and social activities (tickets should never be $10 a couple, but $5 a person). You will also have to challenge your parish to give you a reason why you, having returned, should stay in a local church that obviously has no room for you. As Rev. Greg Friedman says in his fine book *Why Bother With Church?* (get this book if you're single):

> Some see the church as a place which doesn't welcome them. There is little evident concern for their needs once they've been confirmed or finished CCD or graduated from Catholic high school. They have no children, so they have no need for a parish school or religion program. They aren't planning to be married just yet, and perhaps even look on the church's marriage preparation programs as just more bureaucracy invading their personal lives.
>
> Some of the absent [young adult] faces may have given the church a try, only to find it hostile to their particular faith or style of worship. Pastors and parishes may not offer a liturgy which appeals to them. The parish structure may lack a place to become involved, to serve, to feel needed. Programs designed for grade and high schoolers abound; there is often precious little for adult Catholics who aren't raising a family.

The large number of singles is a new phenomenon. It's an unfinished agenda. If you're one of those singles—and one who has returned—there *is* room in the church for you. But in some instances you have to create that room. You may have to tap into your diocesan office for young adults to see what's being offered. You have to find reasons to remain in the church you have returned to (again, read Friedman). You have to bring us into the next century.

As for those who are single because of divorce, know that almost every diocese and parish has some kind of group for divorced and separated Catholics and offers sensitive assistance in seeking annulments. Resources abound and there is no reason that those who have returned home cannot take advantage of them.

Women's Issues

That the Catholic church (like many another) is a "patriarchal" church is a matter of record, but there has been change—and great change in such a short time, considering that all institutions by definition are conservative. For a 2000-year-old institution like the church, as regards women, change has been remarkable. Even back in 1988—and it's increased greatly since—official records showed the following: 17 women were diocesan chancellors, 82 parish administrators, 59 school superintendents, 75 directors of diocesan school programs, 39 heads of family life offices, 28 editors of diocesan newspapers, 22 marriage tribunal judges, and 20 presidents of diocesan pastoral councils. Such positions would have been unthinkable a hundred years ago.

Women today are in every phase of official and unofficial church life. Women are spiritual directors, Scripture scholars, theologians, writers, teachers in seminaries, and students of theology. Presently ordination is closed off to them—some prefer not to be ordained, not to be in that kind of male power structure—but for the most part they still find opportunities for witness and leadership as never before in the church. That such opportunities are uneven is to understate the matter. One woman, a professor of pastoral theology, writes:

During moments of reflection it is not uncommon for women to come to the realization that the church is not a place of liberation but rather a place of oppression. Examples of this abound. A woman works on a parish team, is a member of the local parish council, or is a

Eucharistic minister, and almost overnight discovers that she is no longer allowed to participate in these activities because the priest who supported her has been moved to a different assignment and the new pastor does not believe in collaborative ministry. . . . Women choose different methods for dealing with these experiences. Some leave the church; others continue to participate; some speak out against the injustice they see and are labeled "angry feminists"; some live with the tension by attending church liturgies and women's liturgies; some attempt to be content with the slow progress that they see; some throw themselves into church activities and try to ignore their feelings.
Rosemary Chinnici (*The Catholic World,* Nov.-Dec. 1991)

So it is obvious that there are still conflicts in the male-female relationships in the church as there are in higher education, the military, corporate life, and society in general. Still, great changes have been made (for example, the official use of inclusive language), and what business remains unfinished should not prevent us from seeing what has been and what can be, should not keep us from enjoying the fruits of our return.

One feminist chronicles her return to the church from anger and anti-Catholicism; she attributes it to the influence of a friend who himself had returned to church and invited her in her time of struggle to go to Mass with him. She was amazed at the participation of women at the Mass. She didn't admit it then, but that, along with the experience of praying with others, started her return. Today she writes:

I continue to get angry at what I see as the hypocrisy of the hierarchy; sometimes it seems to me they don't have an inkling of what Jesus was really about. . . . But I've come to understand that this is my church too, and

I intend to reclaim it for my own. . . . We are the church. . . . When my friends ask me why the Catholic church—why not one of the other Christian churches—I can now easily answer them. I have come back to the Catholic church because nowhere else can I celebrate the liturgy with others on a daily basis. Nowhere else can I daily receive the body and blood of Jesus Christ. . . . The eucharist is the primary reason I'm a Catholic.

Karen Ann Speltz (*The Catholic World*, Mar.-Apr. 1993)

Another woman, a convert, writes an article entitled "A Feminist's Path to Rome" and cites both her need for community and her need for Mary.

How can I not love a church which holds Mary as the ideal of normative humanity? Which proclaims so openly that salvation comes into the world in the most basic genital way, through a woman? That her values, not as mother (Jesus was clear about that) but as a human being who is female, are the values that lead to resurrection and the coronation of redeemed humanity?

I am too old, and too well trained by the women's movement, for romantic love. My falling in love is, I trust, not a chosen blindness to the difficulties and weaknesses of the Catholic church, nor a conviction that I can very quickly recreate its character in my own image. But it is love, reasonable love, and it is a joy.

Sara Maitland (*The Tablet*, April 3, 1993)

Sexuality

Standard Catholic teaching on sexuality is as lovely as it is unfinished. Sex, says the church, is both unitive and procreative. It unites two people in love and it tends to go beyond the couple into new life. Such a view of sex demands the respect of permanency and exclusivity. In no other way can we honor one another and provide for children. To take sex from being a unifying factor in love is to turn it into selfish release. To take it from being life-giving in principle is to constrict love. To deny its exclusive property is to sow distrust and construct disposable partners (and thus to make them commodities rather than persons). To deny its permanent property is to scar children for life. All this makes sense, but for many, it falls on deaf ears, including single Catholics who appear to have a higher rate of premarital sex than the general population. And we might add, including the Baby Boomers, 81 percent of whom do not accept the church's teaching on divorce and remarriage.

But the fact is that sex without public commitment, as priest-sociologist Andrew Greeley says, is fraught with dangers of deception, self-deception, and exploitation, particularly of women by men. That's why all the old traditions of every stripe have insisted on chastity for women. Whatever other self-serving reasons may have been present, the fact remains that marital commitment is more important to a woman than to a man. Men greatly benefit, of course, from sex outside of marriage. (The sexual revolution has been by far their boon. It is the women who get pregnant, have illegitimate children, have invasive abortions—with the law having institutionalized the male's irresponsibility, he has no say in any of these options—and diseases that ravage women far more than men.)

Thus, according to all data, women do not benefit from sex outside of marriage (and to this extent, sex between unmarrieds is a form of exploitation). The data shows that outside-of-marriage sex does not provide any measurable greater happiness for women. As Greeley's research concludes: "However much marriage may have been an instrument of oppression, it is certainly obvious . . . that it is the sexual context in which women are most likely to enjoy psychological well-being" ("Sex and the Single Catholic," *America*, November 2, 1992).

The misuse of sex, tearing it from its unifying and creative forces, is one of the tragedies of today. Daily we see the moral, physical, and emotional cost of illegitimate babies—four out of every ten born out of wedlock to single parents—the unconscionable million and a half abortions each year, the well-documented continuing trauma on the children of divorce as well as on the parents, the astronomical financial cost of out-of-wedlock children, and the spread of incurable sexual diseases (one in five in this country have sexually caused viral diseases according to the Alan Guttmacher Institute, with the greatest effect on women and those under 25). Daily we see family life decaying as children younger and younger act out their pain in terrible and unrelenting violence. In other words, there's something to be said about the church's traditional morality of chastity before marriage and fidelity after.

But, of course, there is also unfinished business brought on by modern insights and technology. What about birth control? Why is the church's prohibition so universally rejected among Catholics? Should there not be nuances within the couple's lives that permit it? What about sex between those already betrothed, already publicly committed? How about those who are radically homosexual and cannot live a life of chastity and should not live a life of promiscuity? Is it not better for them to have a stable and faithful partner? We should note that the new *Catechism of the Catholic Church* has at last officially conceded that homosexuality is an involuntary condition, has admitted that some people are constituitively homosexual, and has showed compassion for this condition. Still, the tradition is ambivalent and often hurtful. One devout Catholic homosexual, who is editor of the magazine *The New Republic*, when asked what are the good and positive elements in the Catholic tradition that could lead to a more coherent position on homosexuality, replied:

> Natural law! Here is something [homosexuality] that seems to occur spontaneously in nature, in all societies and civilizations. Why not a teaching about the nature of homosexuality and what its good is. How can we be good? Teach us. How does one inform the moral lives of homosexuals? The church has an obligation to all its faithful to teach us how to live and how to be good— which is not merely a dismissal, silence, embarrassment of a "unique" doctrine on one's inherent disorder. Explain it. How does God make this? Why does it occur? What should we do? How can the doctrine of Christian love be applied to homosexual people as well?
>
> Andrew Sullivan (*America*, May 8, 1993)

It is significant that these questions can be raised publicly in a Catholic magazine; it offers hope that answers will be struggled over. Other questions: Is every single instance in every circumstance of an early abortion sinful? That 68 percent of the Baby Boomers deny that one must obey the church's teaching on abortion shows how wide the gap is and how much dialogue there must yet be. These are questions that have to be continually examined within the framework of great Catholic moral teaching. Sexual morality is part of our unfinished agenda; it requires a continually formed conscience and a great respect for a communal, not merely a personal, context.

Scandals
Finally, all returning Catholics like yourself realize that you have come back to the church, not to the Kingdom of God.

You have come back home to a believing community that has had the wisdom and humility in the past to parade the motto: *Ecclesia semper reformanda* (The church is always in need of reform). Since the church is people, it is imperfect and, as in any family, we live with scandal in low and high places. We live with outdated policies, unreasonable rules, and regressive regulations. We live with backward parishes, outmoded organizations, and counterproductive programs. We live with our own sinfulness. We live with embarrassing Catholics, despotic nuns, dictatorial pastors, and obstructionist bishops.

But still—still—not one of these can obscure the Christ who loves us through our church or the sacramental graces that depend on the Spirit and not on limited human beings. I've always liked what a great layman of the past said—and in my bad moments I often return to his words. This man was Frank Sheed, husband, father, great public speaker, defender of the faith, writer, publisher, and one privy to the faith and foibles of the Catholic church. He wrote:

We are not baptized into the hierarchy; do not receive the cardinals sacramentally; will not spend an eternity in the beatific vision of the pope. St. John Fisher could say in a public sermon, "If the pope will not reform the curia, God will." A couple of years later he laid his head on Henry VIII's block for papal supremacy, followed to the same block by Thomas More, who had spent his youth under the Borgia pope, Alexander VI, lived his early manhood under the Medici pope, Leo X, and died for papal supremacy under Clement VIII, as time-serving a pope as Rome ever had.

Christ is the point. I, myself, admire the present pope but even if I criticized him as harshly as some do, even if his successor proved to be as bad as some of those who have gone before, even if I sometimes find the church as I have to live with it, a pain in the neck, I should still say that nothing a pope could do or say would make me wish to leave the church, although I might well wish that he would leave.

Israel, through its best periods, as through its worst, preserved the truth of God's oneness in a world swarming with gods, and a sense of God's majesty in a world sick with its own pride. So with the church. Under the worst administration we could still learn Christ's truth, receive his life in the sacraments, be in union with him to the limit of our willingness. In awareness of Christ, I can know the church as his mystical body, and we must not make our judgment by the neck's sensitivity to pain.

Conclusion

Returning is a process, part of your journey. Along the way you will run into imperfection. Only those totally out of it are surprised at that. The challenge is to finish up the business God gave you to do and to make a difference. To correct where you can, change what you might, and always to pray, always to be faithful, always to bear witness. You too, after all, as we never tire of saying, are the church.

Resources

A Generation of Seekers by Wade Clark Ross (Harper-SanFrancisco, 1993). A fine study of the Baby Boom generation.

Why Bother With the Church? by Greg Friedman, O.F.M. (St. Anthony Messenger Press, 1988). For singles. Grab this one.

Single in the Church by Kay Collier-Slone (Alban Publications, 1992).

What Women Don't Understand About Men (and vice versa) by

John Carmody (Twenty-Third Publications, 1992). Short, delightful, to the point.

The Catholic Experience by Lawrence Cunningham (Crossroad, 1987). A wonderful book on making sense of the Catholic experience.

America magazine, May 8, 1993. The whole issue is devoted to being gay and Catholic. Well done and insightful.

Chapter 10

JOURNEYING

The Return

The movie *The Return of Martin Guerre* replays an old classic theme of the husband thought dead, a wife innocently remarried, and his return after many years. Older, hardly recognizable, he peers through the window of the old homestead to see his wife seemingly happy with her new life. Should he stay? Should he fade away? Whatever the choice, life had to go on.

You have returned to the church, peered through the window, and have seen some changes, changes we have tried to surface in this short book. Now you have to make a decision. Shall you just "come back" passively and get yourself on the parish rolls and fade into the background, or shall you come back by delving more deeply into the tradition and journeying more profoundly with Jesus and your fellow parishioners? We hope, of course, it's the latter. And so for you we have some final suggestions, some for the head and others for the heart.

Shaping Our Minds and Souls
Would you care if I told you that in 1993 in the United States there were:

+ 1692 television stations with over 5000 channels
+ 12,672 radio stations
+ 1586 newspapers
+ 11,328 magazines

or that the typical American in a year

+ watches 1550 hours of TV
+ listens to 1160 hours of radio on one of 530 million radio sets
+ spends 180 hours reading 94 pounds of newspapers
+ spends 110 hours reading magazines
+ has the opportunity to read the more than 30,000 new books in print each year
+ sees 38,822 commercials or over 100 TV ads per day
+ hears or sees another 100 to 300 more ads on radio, newspapers, and magazines
+ receives 216 pieces of direct mail advertising
+ receives 50 telemarketing phone calls, which contact 7 million people a day
+ plus what he or she sees daily on billboards, posters, T-shirts, bumper stickers, cabs and buses, race cars, tennis tournaments, jazz festivals, and golf matches?

Let's add these facts:

+ Kids under five watch 23 hours of TV a week.
+ High schoolers have already logged 15,000 hours of TV (an activity second only to sleep).
+ Two out of three Americans even watch TV while eating dinner.

+ One out of four adults in a *TV Guide* survey would rather pass up one million dollars than forego TV.

Does it all work? Absolutely! We Americans are only 6 percent of the world population but we consume almost 60 percent of the world's advertising. And if, as they do, manufacturers spend more than $45 billion a year to advertise and another $60 billion on product promotion, you know they intend to get it back and get it back with profit.

Were I writing all this about another country, say, the former Soviet Union, you would immediately—and correctly—think of brainwashing. For what I recounted is a massive, ongoing shaping of our lives and values done in such a subtle and subliminal way that not only do we not realize it, but we actually enjoy it!

Continuing Education

Because, as we have just seen, the mass media are precisely that, mass, we have little inclination and less time to reflect, to critique, to challenge, and to nourish our spiritual lives. Because the media are so massive, what time we do have is filled with images, desires, and activities clearly hostile to the gospel of Jesus. An observer from the secular realm, Norman Lear (the man, you recall, who gave us Archie Bunker, George Jefferson, Fred Sanford, and Mary Hartman), said in an address to the Harvard Business and Divinity Schools:

Most Americans seem to be aware, I believe, that our society has seriously lost its way. Our popular culture celebrates the material and largely ignores the spirit. The 1980s are over—yet greed is still the order of the day in a society preoccupied at all levels with the pursuit of bottom lines, a society which celebrates consumption, careerism, and winning, and lives by the

creed of "I've got mine, Jack." We have become a num-
bers-oriented culture that puts more faith in what we
can see, touch, and hear, and is suspicious of the un-
quantifiable, intuitive, and mysterious—a culture that
has lost touch with the best of its humanity.

Sometimes I wonder if this isn't the root cause of so
much that is wrong on the surface of our society. We
just may be the most well-informed, yet least self-
aware people in history. Whether we live in Kentucky
or Idaho, Los Angeles or New York, the same problems hang out there for all of us to see; we all drink
from the same media trough.

And that "media trough" is a demanding, competing, ongoing brainwashing, a process that molds. It shapes us into
consumers from the time our parents put us in front of the
electronic babysitter. And that's fine by the media, because
these days TV pitches directly to the kids now that mom is
as much away from home as dad. "Kids are making more
and more purchasing decisions," said Arthur I. Pober, director of the Children's Advertising Review Unit of the
Council of Better Business Bureaus. "Because of that, they're
being marketed to directly, and that gives them consumer
power." Research shows evidence of that power: Children
from ages 4 to 12 spent $9 billion in 1991 and teenagers
spent $8.9 billion in 1992. Other studies have shown how
television directly breeds violence into children.

Lest you feel we're getting too far from the point, let me
remind you that all the input and stimulus not only harms
the Christian value system, but also leaves little time for the
intellectual and formative life of the spirit. It saps the time
from the contemplative life and that contemplative life is
more and more a deep desire for today's people like yourself. The irony is that we Catholics have a stupendous trad-

tion of mysticism and contemplation, which we have preserved through the centuries. There are many fine courses
and available books and seminars on spirituality. And there
are more and more spiritual centers and directors available
for everyone. But this means the discipline of reading, stud-
ying, praying, and meditating. In a word, now that you
have returned, reclaim your heritage. Subscribe to Catholic
magazines (I've listed some in the resources) and read spiritual books. Mark your calendar for a retreat. Attend short
seminars. We really do have a deep and abiding spiritual
treasure. Returning means tapping into it once again.

Singing Along with Jesus

Even as you continue your religious education, you realize
that you can't believe everything. Yet you still have a voice.
Let me explain that by using some imagery. One of my fa-
vorite feasts is that of All Saints. I picture this feast in terms
of a mighty chorus of all those endless 144 thousands of
people (biblical talk for infinity: 12 is a perfect number in ancient lore, and so 12 x 12 which = 144 is perfection times perfection, or fullness times fullness). We all belong to that
chorus: the saints in heaven, the soon-to-be saints in pur-
gatory, and the saints now on Earth and we're all belting
out our heavenly song. Yet there are two truths to remember.

The first is this: No one believes it all. Each of us in the
chorus is gifted with only a partial understanding of the
mystery of God and the church. And so in our large chorus,
one sings with great intensity and serene faith. Another
sings with little heart and with severe doubts. Or we sing
fulsomely today because emotionally and spiritually we
happen to be in a good place. But another time, in another
mental or emotional state, we feel distant and distracted and
can hardly get the words out of our dry mouths. No one believes it all, but *together we sing more than we can sing alone.*

Remember: Together we sing more than we can sing alone. Others in the chorus sing with us and sing extra loud at our faltering and stumbling places. Our shared singing amplifies and completes our partial faith. Others fill in for our hesitation. Others sing what we cannot and believe those sections we cannot accept. No one believes it all—but all believe.

The second truth to remember is this: If no one believes it all, so also no one believes all the time. Our faith journey is seldom smooth and uninterrupted. At times it fluctuates between belief and unbelief. Tragedy—for example, the death of a child or the death of a marriage—can break one's trust in God. Meanwhile? Meanwhile the community of faith sings verses such as one cannot sing. The community chorus sustains such people until they can come to faith once more.

Your parish community is like that. We sing for one another and supply strength for one another's weaknesses. Others sing when you and I are unable or unwilling. Think of our tradition: Peter singing for Thomas in his doubts, Thomas singing for Peter in his sin, Monica singing for her son Augustine when he was in his period of sinfulness and unbelief, Clare singing for Francis when he was sad. No one believes it all and no one believes all the time—that's why a faith community is so important on our journey.

A Dislocated Journey

Some who have returned still carry two burdens. One is that they still feel that there are some things in their lives that are completely out of harmony with the church or church policy. Such burdens might be a marriage outside the church or practicing birth control or a past experience of an abortion. Another is carrying some guilt around from the past, some terrible deed or unkindness we did to another—and especially if we can't apologize since that person is dead. Such burdens restrict the joy of returning home.

The solution to the first is to come home anyway, take part in Mass with the community, pray, and talk with a priest. The solution to the second is to remember Jesus over and over again. To recall his mission of forgiveness and his story of the Prodigal Son, his reaching out to the Good Thief, and his very first act after his resurrection: He breathed on his apostles and said, "Receive the Holy Spirit. Whose sins you shall forgive, they are forgiven them." For anyone so troubled I recommend Brennan Manning's book, *A Stranger to Self-Hatred* (Dimension Books, 1982).

Guideposts for the Journey

Finally, I suggest a few guideposts for your continuing journey in the church:

1. *Reflect on what brought you back.* Very few people are drawn to the faith either the first time or the second time by figuring out the Trinity. Rather, people come to faith by lovely things: the birth of a child, the wonderment of the world, a kindness done, a hero observed, a trauma endured. This is a way of saying that such reflection or prayer is an essential ingredient to staying on course.

2. *Pray for greater faith.* As we said, you're somewhere in the chorus.You might make your own Thomas Merton's famous prayer:

My Lord God, I have no idea where I am going. I do not see the road ahead of me. I cannot know for certain where it will end. Nor do I really know myself, and the fact that I think I am doing your will does not mean that I am actually doing so. But I believe the desire to please you actually does please you. And I hope that I have had that desire in all that I am doing. I hope that I will do nothing apart from that desire. And I know that if I do this you will lead me by the right road though I know nothing about it. Therefore will I trust you always though I may seem to be lost and in the shadow of death. I will not fear, for you are ever with me, and you will never leave me to face my perils alone. Amen.

3. *Attend liturgy faithfully.* I don't like the phrase "going to church." It always sounds to me like going to a club or going to school. I mean, rather, join in the community worship every Sunday. You and your family need the support of the others (chorus), their prayers, example, and fellowship— and they need yours. You should give witness to your neighbors and take time out to say out loud *somewhere* what society does not permit: that Jesus Christ is Lord.

4. *Read the Bible.* You can get small pocket copies of the New Testament. If you drive to work, the whole Bible is on audiocassette. Join a bible study group. In short, get grounded in the word of God.

Conclusion

We have a custom in our parish. Once a year we have our Oliver Celebration. On this occasion we invite all those who have joined the parish in the past year to a party. There we welcome them once more, have them introduce themselves to one another, have the various ministries make their pitch to them, and then give each one a piece of a puzzle. Actually, the puzzle is a photograph of our church that we had blown up and jigsawed. Each family or member puts a piece in place till the puzzle is completed. The symbolism is obvious: Each of us makes up a community. Then we have refreshments and give them a little green plant before they go, another symbol of living growth. But I want to return to the name, Oliver Celebration. That, you might recall, is the name of a musical based on Dickens's novel *Oliver Twist*. One of the hit songs in the musical has these lyrics:

Consider yourself at home;
consider yourself part of the family;
consider yourself one of us.

And that's exactly what we wanted to convey. And that's exactly what this book wants to convey. Welcome home!

Resources

Annulment: Your Chance to Remarry Within the Catholic Church by Joseph Zwack (HarperSanFrancisco, 1983). Helpful.

Silence on Fire by William H. Shannon (Crossroad, 1993). A grand, sensible book on prayer.

Faith Rediscovered: Coming Home to Catholicism by Lawrence Cunningham (Paulist Press, 1987). A short book to share.

Do Children Need Religion? by Martha Fay (Pantheon Books, 1993). If you're a parent, read this along with *Today's Children* by David Hamburg, M.D. (Time Books, 1992).

Believing: Understanding the Creed by Gerard O'Collins and Mary Venturini (Paulist Press, 1991).

Catholic Customs and Traditions by Greg Dues (Twenty-Third Publications, rev. ed., 1991) Must reading, and rewarding.

Some selected magazines that are worth having in your house. These reflect, of course, my tastes and biases. There are many more, but I don't want to overload you.

U.S. Catholic (205 W. Monroe St., Chicago IL 60606). A good, all around, award-winning magazine that is always current and challenging. For general audiences.

St. Anthony Messenger (St. Anthony Messenger Press, 1615 Republic St., Cincinnati OH 45210). Same as above.

Salt (same address as *U.S. Catholic*). A magazine "for Christians who seek social justice."

America (P.O. Box 48468, Atlanta GA 30362). Always relevant and challenging.

Commonweal (15 Dutch St., New York NY 10038). A more indepth magazine. Provocative and timely.

The Catholic World (997 MacArthur Blvd., Mahwah NJ 07439). Treats well one subject an issue.

The Family (50 St. Paul's Ave., Boston MA 02130). One of the several family-centered magazines.

The Liguorian (Liguori MO 63057). A small, general magazine.

New Oxford Review (Room 85, 1069 Kains Ave., Berkeley CA 94706). A good, conservative magazine.

First Things (The Institute on Religion and Public Life, 156 Fifth Ave., New York NY 10010). Same as above.

Of Related Interest...

Catholic Customs & Traditions
A Popular Guide
Greg Dues
Practices and curiosities that have become part of the Catholic heritage
over the years are explained here.

ISBN: 0-89622-515-1, 224 pp, $9.95

Faith Alive
A New Presentation of Catholic Belief and Practice
edited by Rowanne Pasco & John Redford
This is a panoramic view of the Catholic Church, its teachings and
traditions. A contemporary, in-depth portrait.

ISBN: 0-89622-408-2, 320 pp, $9.95

Nicene Creed
Poetic Words for a Prosaic World
Stephen C. Rowan
An ideal introduction to the Creed for catechumens and for teens
preparing for confirmation. Questions for study and reflection included.

ISBN: 0-89622-451-1, 80 pp, $5.95

Sacraments Alive
Their History, Celebration and Significance
Sandra DeGidio
This book updates readers' understanding of the sacraments as they are
celebrated today.

ISBN: 0-89622-489-9, 160 pp, $7.95

This Is Our Mass
Tom Coyle
The rich scriptural origins and liturgical development of our eucharistic
celebration are explored in this book.

ISBN: 0-89622-394-9, 149 pp, $5.95

Available at religious bookstores or from

TWENTY-THIRD PUBLICATIONS
P.O. Box 180 • Mystic, CT 06355
1-800-321-0411